A Multimedia Course in the Catholic Faith
Based on the *Catechism of the Catholic Church*

PARTICIPANT'S BOOK

A Written Summary of the Teaching Content of the EVANGELIUM Presentations

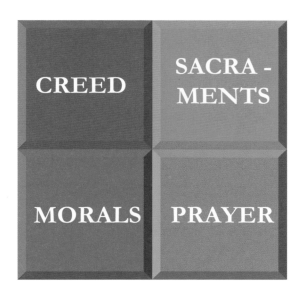

CREED

SACRA-MENTS

MORALS

PRAYER

Fr Marcus Holden MA (Oxon), STL

Archdiocese of Southwark

Fr Andrew Pinsent MA (Oxon), DPhil, STB, PhL, PhD

Diocese of Arundel and Brighton

Catholic Truth Society

Nihil obstat: Father Anton Cowan, Censor.
Imprimatur: Rt Rev. Alan Hopes, VG, Auxiliary Bishop in Westminster,
Westminster, 3rd July 2006, Feast of St Thomas, Apostle.

The *Nihil obstat* and *Imprimatur* are a declaration that a book or pamphlet is considered to be free from doctrinal or moral error. It is not implied that those who have granted the *Nihil obstat* and *Imprimatur* agree with the contents, opinions or statements expressed.

Acknowledgements

The authors extend their thanks to the Catholic Truth Society, especially the members of the editorial board and staff who encouraged the development of EVANGELIUM from a catechetical course delivered at the Venerable English College in Rome to a published product: the Rt Rev. Paul Hendricks, Mr Fergal Martin, Fr Peter Edwards, Ms Glynn Johnson, Mr Pierpaolo Finaldi, Mr Richard Brown and Mr Stephen Campbell. They also thank the professors of the Pontifical Gregorian University, in particular Fr Kevin Flannery SJ, Emeritus Dean of Philosophy, and Fr Joseph Carola SJ, Professor of Patristic Theology, for their detailed reviews of the theological and philosophical content. They express their gratitude to Fr Michel Remery, Fr Bruno Witchalls, Fr John Flynn, Fr Christopher Miller, Fr James Mackay, Fr David Charters, Mr Neil Brett, and the members of the 'Bellarmine Project' for their reviews and suggestions. The authors also acknowledge those who have encouraged, promoted and co-operated on this project in a multitude of ways, including the Most Rev. Raymond Burke, Fr Tim Finigan, Fr Mark Vickers, Fr Nicholas Schofield, Fr Richard Whinder, Fr Richard Biggerstaff, Fr Stephen Langridge and Prof. Eleonore Stump. The authors also thank their parents, John and Irene Holden and Charles and Teresa Pinsent, for their on-going moral support, prayers and advice.

Other Evangelium Resources
Evangelium Presenter's Guide, ISBN 978 1 86082 394 7; CTS Code EV2; Published 2006, revised 2009
Evangelium CDRom, CTS Code EV3; Published 2006, revised 2009

Contents

The Baptism of Christ by Piero della Francesca

This picture reminds us of the teaching of the gospel - that all people are called to follow Christ.
Like the catechumen in the background of this picture, we too are called to leave behind our sinful ways of
life to follow Christ, who is in the foreground, along the path of discipleship to the kingdom of heaven.

Introduction

Go into all the world and preach the gospel to the whole creation.

Mark 16:15

eVANGELIUM

What is 'EVANGELIUM'?

'Evangelium' means 'gospel' or 'good news'. This course is called EVANGELIUM because it aims to teach the good news of our salvation in Jesus Christ.

Aim of EVANGELIUM

The EVANGELIUM multimedia catechetical course teaches the essentials of Catholic faith and life in a straightforward, precise and attractive manner. The course is based on the *Catechism of the Catholic Church* and the materials are organised in the same fourfold way: Creed, Sacraments, Morals and Prayer.

Those who with God's help have welcomed Christ's call and freely responded to it are urged on by love of Christ to proclaim the Good News everywhere in the world. This treasure, received from the apostles, has been faithfully guarded by their successors. All Christ's faithful are called to hand it on from generation to generation, by professing the faith, by living it in fraternal sharing, and by celebrating it in liturgy and prayer.

Catechism of the Catholic Church par. 3 (Prologue)

Who is EVANGELIUM for?

EVANGELIUM is for all those who wish to deepen their knowledge of the Catholic Faith, whether or not they are practising members of the Church.

The course materials are intended principally for those participating in the *Rite of Christian Initiation for Adults* (RCIA) or other adult catechetical programs. Other uses include Confirmation preparation, youth catechesis, marriage preparation and self-instruction. The study of the course materials can be carried out in classes, in small groups or by individuals.

The aim of this Participant's Book

The principal aim of this *Participant's Book* is to assist each person taking part in an EVANGELIUM course; it summarises the course presentations and provides additional references for further reading.

This *Participant's Book* can also be used independently of any course, as a complete, attractive and concise summary of the key teachings of the Catholic Faith.

Teaching an EVANGELIUM session using a PC projector, one way in which the course can be used by groups, such as RCIA candidates

BENEFITS OF EVANGELIUM

- Concise, precise wording to communicate key ideas in a timely manner

- The use of computer based presentations to animate and link concepts and images

- Quotations from Scripture, the *Catechism* and other Catholic sources to illustrate and explain

- Suggested further reading and activities to reinforce learning

- A modular approach: each session can stand alone to provide maximum course flexibility

- Beautiful religious art to convey a rich visual experience of the key persons and ideas

The centuries-old conciliar tradition teaches us that images are also a preaching of the Gospel. Artists in every age have offered the principal facts of the mystery of salvation to the contemplation and wonder of believers by presenting them in the splendour of colour and in the perfection of beauty. It is an indication of how today more than ever, in a culture of images, a sacred image can express much more than what can be said in words, and be an extremely effective and dynamic way of communicating the Gospel message.

Pope Benedict XVI, Introduction to the *Compendium of the Catechism.*

The order of the sessions

The order of the sessions in this *Participant's Book* follows the main fourfold division of the *Catechism*.

Creed	Sacraments	Morals	Prayer
10	5	5	5

Since each session is a complete lesson in itself, the order in which the sessions are presented is flexible and should be adapted to the needs of participants. Page 51 of this book shows a possible sequence of sessions to accompany the *Rite of Christian Initiation for Adults* (RCIA). Page 52 presents an alternative sequence for general purpose catechesis.

The estimated time required for teaching a session using the CD is 1 hour 10 minutes.

Viewing EVANGELIUM presentations on a laptop, one way in which the course can be used for personal study

Praying and living the Gospel

EVANGELIUM seeks to impart much more than information. Although it is possible to know about the Catholic Faith using human reason alone, to *know* the faith with a kind of inner illumination of its truth is a gift from God. It is important to ask God to impart and increase this gift of faith.

It is therefore highly recommended to begin and end each session with a prayer. Page vii offers a suitable prayer of St Thomas Aquinas; others are provided in the *Presenter's Guide* and the course presentations.

To know the faith also involves experiencing and living the faith. Catholic art, prayers and practical suggestions are included in this course to encourage and nurture this experience and life of grace.

Course materials and sources

EVANGELIUM COURSE MATERIALS

- *Presentations on CD*. A self-starting CD with twenty-five PowerPoint Viewer© presentations.
- *Participant's Book*. A written summary of the content of the presentations.
- *Presenter's Guide*. A guide to presenting the sessions with further references and activities.

The main reference sources for EVANGELIUM are Scripture and the *Catechism*. Scripture citations are generally taken from the Revised Standard Version (RSV) Catholic Edition. Citations from other standard translations are used occasionally when an alternative translation highlights a particular point more clearly. On such occasions, the alternative translation is indicated by an abbreviation.

The following tables list the Bible translations and Biblical books cited in EVANGELIUM:

BIBLE TRANSLATIONS USED IN EVANGELIUM

No abbreviation	Revised Standard Version
NRSV	New Revised Standard Version
NJB	New Jerusalem Bible
DRA	Douay-Rheims Bible
KJV	King James Version

BIBLICAL BOOK ABBREVIATIONS

Gen	Genesis	1 Cor	1 Corinthians
Ex	Exodus	2 Cor	2 Corinthians
Deut	Deuteronomy	Eph	Ephesians
Isa	Isaiah	Col	Colossians
Mt	Gospel of Matthew	Jas	James
Mk	Gospel of Mark	1 Pet	1 Peter
Lk	Gospel of Luke	2 Pet	2 Peter
Jn	Gospel of John	1 Jn	1 John
Rom	Romans	Rev	Revelation

References to the *Catechism of the Catholic Church* are indicated by "ccc." followed by the paragraph number. The reference "ccc. 50", for example, indicates paragraph 50 of the *Catechism*.

The majority of other citations are sources cited by the *Catechism*. In such cases, both the original source and the *Catechism* reference are provided.

The time is fulfilled, and the kingdom of God is at hand; repent, and believe in the gospel.　　Mk 1:15

The Magdalene Reading by Rogier van der Weyden

Opening Prayer

As the final goal of Christian teaching is to know God, it is good to ask for God's help at the beginning of each session. The following short prayer is from St Thomas Aquinas, who always prayed before study.

Bestow upon me, O God,
an understanding that knows you, wisdom
in finding you, a way of life that is
pleasing to you, perseverance that faithfully
waits for you, and confidence that I shall
embrace you at the last. Amen.

The Church in glory: detail from *The Last Judgment* by Fra Angelico

This symbolic representation of the kingdom of heaven reminds us of the happiness God desires us to have as the true goal and meaning of our lives: to be gathered into heaven where we shall see the face of God, in the company and friendship of the angels and saints in everlasting glory.

The Meaning of Life

Let the hearts of those who seek the LORD rejoice!
Psalm 105:3

*e*VANGELIUM

> The meaning of life refers to the most fundamental reasons for the existence of the world and ourselves.

Why?

As a child grows up, the most persistent question he or she will tend to ask is 'why?' As human beings we not only ask what things are but also why they are. The Greek philosopher Aristotle said that this desire is universal, *"All people by nature desire to know!"*

The question 'why?' can also be applied to the whole universe and to human beings. Why is the universe here? Why are we here? What is the goal of human life? Men and women throughout history have attempted to answer these questions.

What is the 'first be-cause'?

All the things we see in the universe are caused by other things. Many thinkers have concluded that this chain of causes cannot go on forever. There must be a 'first be-cause', a necessary, eternal and unchanging 'first cause' which creates and sustains everything. This first cause is what people naturally call 'God'.

In addition, the universe shows evidence of many processes that are ordered towards things of great complexity and beauty. This order and goodness encourages belief in a God who created them.

What is 'God'?

'God' is what people rationally call the first cause and purpose of things, but this raises questions about what God is and God's relationship with us.

For Aristotle, 'God' was the unmoved mover. For Plato, he was the unchanging good. For Anselm, he was *'that greater than which nothing can be conceived'*. For Newton, he was the architect of the laws of nature.

All rational models of the cosmos also require a 'first be-cause'. Einstein, for example, often referred to the first cause of the intelligibility of the universe using the language of 'God' or the 'mind of God'.

The School of Athens by Raphael Sanzio

> *Question the beauty of the earth, question the beauty of the sea ... question all these realities. All respond: 'See, we are beautiful'. Their beauty is a confession. These beauties are subject to change. Who made them if not the Beautiful One who is not subject to change?* St Augustine, Sermon 241 (ccc. 32)

What does creation teach us about God?

From what has been created, we can learn that God is one, all powerful, all good and unchanging.

MISTAKES ABOUT GOD	
☒ **Polytheism**	Denies the one God in favour of many 'gods'. This is wrong since there can only be one first cause; several gods would introduce chaos and unintelligibility into creation.
☒ **Pantheism**	Denies that God is distinct from the world. This is wrong because the first cause is unchangeable, unlike all the other beings of creation.
☒ **A powerless 'god'**	Denies that God is all-powerful. This is wrong because the first cause must have the power to cause everything in creation.
☒ **An evil 'god'**	Denies that God is good. This is wrong because what God has created is good. Evil in the world always refers to the corruption of some intrinsically good thing.

> *For since the creation of the world God's invisible qualities – his eternal power and divine nature – have been clearly seen, being understood from what has been made.*
> Romans 1:20 NIV

What are Human Beings?

The Creation of Adam by Michelangelo

Human beings differ from all other living beings on earth. Although we are animals, we also have the capacity *to know* and to communicate intelligently using *language*. Aristotle calls us 'rational animals'.

The kind of knowledge we have is also unique. It is not just sensory perception and habit, but the knowledge of *what* and *why* a thing is. Without this capacity we would have no science or philosophy.

In addition, human beings have a unique ability *to choose*, which gives rise to an enormous variety of human work and action, both good and evil.

Many philosophers have realised that the kind of being who *knows* and *chooses* in this way must have some quality which cannot simply be reduced to mere matter that is subject to change and decay. They therefore infer that we have immortal souls that do not perish when our bodies die.

What do we want?

People seem to want many different things in life. However, when the deeper question is asked about what we really want, St Augustine answers that in all things we are really searching for happiness.

> *We all want to live happily; in the whole human race there is no one who does not assent to this.*
> St Augustine, *De moribus eccl.* I, 3, 4 (ccc. 1718)

We therefore look for happiness. Proper happiness is something complete, fulfilling, pleasurable, and permanent. Although in this life we experience many partial and temporary joys, none of these truly bring happiness. Furthermore, there is much pain and suffering in life, and our bodies decay and die.

Where is happiness found?

Given our mortality, together with much suffering and discontent in life, it is clear that permanent happiness is impossible for us without some help beyond ourselves. Even though our souls may be immortal, we lose everything else when we die.

Knowing that there is a good God, human beings have rightly looked to God to fulfil their hope for happiness. Furthermore, as naturally religious beings it is clear that happiness must involve *knowing* God as the first cause and reason for all things.

> *You have made us for yourself and our hearts are restless till they rest in you.*
> St Augustine, *Confessions*, I.1.1 (ccc. 30; cf. 1718)

What does God offer us?

Christianity affirms God's goodness and desire for our happiness. In Jesus Christ, however, God offers us what is infinitely greater: a sharing in his own divine life and blessedness.

> *God, infinitely perfect and blessed in himself, in a plan of sheer goodness freely created man to make him share in his own blessed life.*
> *Compendium of the Catechism of the Catholic Church*, question 1

Due to this higher calling, God never allows us to be satisfied with anything less. It is only by responding to this invitation of friendship with God that we also find our natural happiness and fulfilment. St Paul speaks of this great gift and promise as follows:

> *What no eye has seen, nor ear heard, nor the human heart conceived, what God has prepared for those who love him.*
> 1 Cor 2:9 NRSV

The Greek word εὐαγγέλιον (in Latin, 'evangelium') means 'good news' or 'gospel'. The good news of Christianity is that God has made it possible, through Jesus Christ, for us to enjoy this new life and be happy with him for ever. This course, also called 'Evangelium', has been written to enable people to know and grow in this new life.

> *These are written that you may believe that Jesus is the Christ, the Son of God, and that believing you may have life in his name.*
> Jn 20:31

References

Catechism of the Catholic Church:
ccc. 27-49 (*Compendium* questions 1-5)

Further reading:
HAFFNER, P., *The Mystery of Reason*, Gracewing; CREAN, T., *God is No Delusion: A Refutation of Richard Dawkins*, Ignatius Press. DAVIES, B., *An Introduction to the Philosophy of Religion*, Oxford University Press

Creation and Fall

In the beginning God created the heavens and the earth.
Genesis 1:1

What is Creation?

Creation is the special act by which God freely creates all things that exist out of nothing.

The Expulsion from Paradise by Giovanni di Paolo

What do philosophy and science say?

Philosophy shows that the universe has a necessary cause, but cannot tell us if the universe has always existed. According to the 'Big Bang' theory (first proposed by a Catholic priest, Monsignor Georges Lemaître), the universe developed from a compact, primitive and fiery state. Science, however, cannot investigate causes beyond the physical universe.

God, however, has revealed that the universe had a beginning and was created 'out of nothing' – out of no other pre-existing thing, *"In the beginning, God created the heavens and the earth"* (Gen 1:1).

What is special about human beings?

Scripture testifies that human beings are unique in having a material body and a spiritual soul, and that each soul is *directly* created by God. Human beings are *persons*, not merely things or even animals, and are therefore of the greatest worth and dignity.

The account in Genesis is not a scientific treatise, but is God's way of revealing to us certain truths about creation and our origins. It reveals that at some point in time God created one man and one woman with a material body and, uniquely among animals, a spiritual soul. In Genesis these parents of the human race are called Adam, meaning 'man', and Eve, *"the mother of all those who live"* (Gen 1:20). This teaching does not exclude the possible evolution of the human body from already existing and living matter. While science has not reached a final conclusion on our biological origins, modern genetics has confirmed that the human race is a single, close genetic family.

What was the first state of human beings?

God has revealed that he created Adam and Eve *without defect* and with special gifts:

- Freedom from disordered desires.
- Bodily immortality.
- Freedom from suffering.
- Extraordinary gifts of knowledge.

Above all, God gave them grace, enabling them to enjoy his intimate friendship. This relationship was to culminate in the perfect and lasting vision of God.

All these gifts and graces *should* have been passed on to the whole human race, including ourselves.

KINDS OF CREATED BEINGS	SPIRITUAL	LIVING	MATERIAL
Angels	☑	☑	
Human beings	☑	☑	☑
Animals		☑	☑
Plants		☑	☑
Other physical beings			☑

Then God said, "Let us make man in our image, after our likeness; ..." So God created man in his own image, in the image of God he created him; male and female he created them.
Genesis 1:26 – 27

3

What is the Fall?

The Fall is the historical event of the first parents of the human race freely choosing to disobey God and thereby suffering serious consequences for themselves and all subsequent generations.

What was the event of the Fall?

God's revelation confirms that at the root of all the world's disorder is an *actual, personal* sin of mankind's first parents. The event of the Fall is revealed by God and presented in the book of Genesis (the first book of the Bible) in a figurative way. Echoes of this reality can also be found in the Creation accounts of other ancient cultures which refer, not just to sin in general, but to an actual, historical event.

The Church teaches that this Fall of human beings followed the Fall of a certain number of purely spiritual beings called angels. The leader of the rebel angels (demons), the devil, is depicted as the serpent of the book of Genesis who tempted our first parents to imitate his own disobedience.

The choice presented to human beings was to make one simple act of loyalty to God.

The serpent or devil, however, tempted our first parents with a lie and they disobeyed God.

The Garden of Eden
by Jacob de Backer

God said: "*You may freely eat of every tree of the garden; but of the tree of the knowledge of good and evil you shall not eat, for in the day that you eat of it you shall die.*"

The devil said: "*You will not die. For God knows that when you eat of it your eyes will be opened, and you will be like God, knowing good and evil.*"

The Original Sin: *So when the woman saw that the tree was good for food, and that it was a delight to the eyes, and that the tree was to be desired to make one wise, she took of its fruit and ate; and she also gave some to her husband, and he ate.*

Gen 2:17; 3:1-5; 3:6

What were the effects of the Fall?

The sin of Adam and Eve was very great because of their perfect creation, with so many gifts and graces, and because they were the parents of the human race.

Detail from *The Expulsion from Paradise* by Giovanni di Paolo

By their sin, Adam and Eve lost:

- Their extraordinary gifts and perfect state.
- Their friendship with God in grace.
- The promise of future glory.

As descendents of Adam (cf. 1 Cor 15:22), we inherit:

- *Original Sin* – the guilt of his sin as father of our race.
- *Evil concupiscence and disorder* – a life of suffering, ignorance and discontent ending in death.
- *A state without grace* – a life without union with God and with no promise of heaven.

Was there hope after the Fall?

Unlike the fallen angels, the human race would not be lost forever. God in his mercy promised a means of salvation from sin and death.

In God's plan of salvation history, there would one day be a new Adam and a second Eve.

"*And I will put enmity between you and the woman, and between your offspring and hers; he will crush your head, and you will strike his heel.*"

Gen 3:15

Madonna with Serpent by Caravaggio

References

Catechism of the Catholic Church:
ccc. 279-421 (*Compendium* questions 51-78)

Further reading:
RATZINGER, J., *In the Beginning: A Catholic Understanding of the Story of Creation and the Fall*, Eerdmans; DUBAY, T., *The Evidential Power of Beauty*, Ignatius Press

Salvation History

In you all the families of the earth shall be blessed.
Genesis 12:3

*e*VANGELIUM

What is Salvation History?

Salvation history is the progressive unfolding of God's plan to save the human race from sin and death after the Fall. This plan gives the true meaning to the entire history of the world.

What are the stages of salvation history?

After the Fall, human beings lost their friendship with God and suffered from sin and death. Through a series of covenants, related in the Old Testament, God gradually re-established a bond with humanity, promised many blessings and a future salvation.

DATE	PATRIARCH or PROPHET	GOD'S PROMISE
Early	**Noah**	The preservation of the world
c. 2000 BC	**Abraham**	The establishment of a chosen people
c. 1450 or c. 1250 BC	**Moses**	The permanent gift of a law and a land
c. 1000 BC	**David**	The founding of an everlasting kingdom
c. 900 – 400 BC	**Prophets**	The coming of a final salvation
c. 20 AD	**John the Baptist**	The coming of the saviour or *Messiah*

The deeper reason for each of these divine promises was to prefigure and prepare the way for the coming of Jesus Christ; the Messiah who would bring a full and final salvation to Israel and to the whole world.

"Everything written about me in the law of Moses and the prophets and the psalms must be fulfilled." Then he opened their minds to understand the scriptures, and said to them, "Thus it is written, that the Christ should suffer and on the third day rise from the dead, and that repentance and forgiveness of sins should be preached in his name to all nations, beginning from Jerusalem." Luke 24:44-47

God's covenant with Noah

GENESIS 6:1-9:17

The human race became more wicked and violent following the Fall, but one man, Noah, won God's favour. God told Noah to build an ark to save his family and preserve certain animals from a flood that was to punish and cleanse the world.

After the flood, God established a covenant with Noah, promising to preserve life until the end of time, giving us the opportunity to be saved.

God's promise to Noah was perfectly fulfilled in Christ who remains with us *"to the end of time"* (Mt 28:20 NJB). Noah's ark prefigures the Church of Christ that carries the faithful to salvation.

God's covenant with Abraham

GENESIS 12:1-3; 17:1-9; 22:1-18

The Sacrifice of Isaac by Caravaggio

God called Abraham to leave his own country. He promised to give him a land, to make him a nation and to bless the whole world through him. Abraham had faith in these promises. He became the father of the Jewish people and settled in the Promised Land.

God's promise to Abraham was perfectly fulfilled in Christ. Through him, God has established a redeemed nation, the Church, given us an everlasting homeland, heaven, and blessed all peoples.

Even when he disobeyed you and lost your friendship you did not abandon him to the power of death ... Again and again you offered a covenant to man.
The Mass (Roman Missal), Eucharistic Prayer IV

What was God's covenant through Moses?

EXODUS 6; EXODUS 19-20; EXODUS 24

Abraham's son Isaac was the father of Jacob whose twelve sons became the fathers of the twelve tribes of Israel. It was from this line that Jesus Christ, the saviour of the world, was finally born.

The eleven sons of Jacob followed Joseph, their brother, into Egypt at a time of famine. The Israelites remained there and grew greatly in number. As a consequence, centuries later, the Egyptians saw them as a threat and began to use them as slaves.

God raised up a leader, Moses, by whom he freed the people of Israel from slavery, gave them his law and brought them to the Promised Land.

Crossing the Red Sea by Cosimo Rosselli

God's work through Moses was perfectly fulfilled by Jesus, who freed us from the slavery of sin and gave the new law of grace. He founded his Church, the new Israel, on twelve apostles to bring us to our Promised Land of heaven.

What was God's covenant with David?

2 SAMUEL 7

The Israelites conquered the Promised Land but broke God's law, repeatedly falling into sin and disasters. They became jealous of surrounding nations and demanded that the judge Samuel give them a king.

After the unfaithfulness of Saul, the first king of Israel, God chose David as king. God promised David that one of his descendents would be established as king forever.

God's promise to David was perfectly fulfilled in Jesus Christ, the Son of David and King of the New Israel, whose reign will never end.

What did the prophets promise?

ISAIAH 53, EZEKIEL 36; JEREMIAH 32:36-42

David's son Solomon built the Temple but broke the commandments. His successors divided his kingdom between north and south. In subsequent centuries the northern kingdom was destroyed. Finally, in 597 BC, Jerusalem and the southern kingdom were captured by the Babylonians who deported many of its people to Babylon.

Throughout this period, God sent prophets such as Elijah, Isaiah, Jeremiah and Ezekiel. These called the people to repentance, justice and peace. They also prophesised a future salvation, a new and everlasting covenant, a Messiah or 'Christ', and a 'suffering servant', who would bear the sins of many.

God's promise of salvation, made through his prophets, was perfectly fulfilled in the Passion, death and Resurrection of Jesus Christ.

Who did John the Baptist herald?

THE BEGINNING OF THE FOUR GOSPELS

Although the people returned from Babylon, there was no new king. They remained at the mercy of the Persians, the Greeks and finally the Romans.

Finally, a last prophet appeared known as John the Baptist. He called the people to repentance and to prepare for the imminent coming of the Messiah.

God's promise, made through John the Baptist, of the coming of the Christ was perfectly fulfilled when John saw Jesus himself and declared of him:

"Behold, the Lamb of God,
who takes away the sin of the world!"

Jn 1:29

References

Catechism of the Catholic Church:
ccc. 50-64 (*Compendium* questions 6-8; 102)

Further reading:
HAHN, S., *A Father who Keeps His Promises*, Servant Publications; SCHOEMAN, R., *Salvation is from the Jews: The Role of Judaism in Salvation History from Abraham to the Second Coming*, Ignatius Press

The Incarnation

The Word became flesh and dwelt among us, full of grace and truth.
John 1:14

*e*VANGELIUM

What is the Incarnation?

By the word 'Incarnation' we mean that God the Son took to himself a human nature like our own.

The word 'Incarnation' expresses the fact that Jesus Christ is not merely a man, a perfect man or even a saint, but God himself become man for our salvation.

How did Jesus Christ come to be born?

The Annunciation is the historical event when God the Father, through the angel Gabriel, asked the Virgin Mary to become the mother of his Son.

"Hail, O favoured one, the Lord is with you! ... Do not be afraid, Mary, for you have found favour with God. And behold, you will conceive in your womb and bear a son, and you shall call his name Jesus."
Lk 1:28-31

Mary, who was and remained a virgin, questioned how she could conceive a child. The angel answered that this child would be conceived through a miracle:

"The Holy Spirit will come upon you, and the power of the Most High will overshadow you; therefore the child to be born will be called holy, the Son of God."
Lk 1:35

Mary gave her free consent to become the Mother of God, opening the way to our salvation:

And Mary said, "Behold, I am the handmaid of the Lord; let it be to me according to your word."
Lk 1:38

The angel of the Lord also appeared to Joseph, Mary's betrothed, assuring him that this child was born of God and to take Mary home as his wife.

At the time of a census called by the Roman Emperor Augustus, Jesus was born in Joseph's home town of Bethlehem, the City of David. Here the king of kings was born in the poverty of a stable. His birth was heralded by a miraculous appearance of angels to nearby shepherds, and a star in the heavens which guided wise men to him.

The Annunciation by Fra Angelico

She gave birth to her first-born son and wrapped him in swaddling cloths, and laid him in a manger.
Lk 2:4-7

What are the titles of Jesus Christ?

Jesus	This is a Hebrew name meaning 'God saves', expressing well in itself the purpose of the Incarnation.
Christ	This is from the Greek *christos*, meaning 'anointed one', a title of a priest, prophet or king. This word was used by the Jews for the promised *Messiah*.
Lord	This is from the Greek *kyrios*, often used for addressing God in the Bible.
Son of God	This is a title of the Messiah and also indicates the divinity of Jesus Christ.
Son of Man	This is a title of the Messiah and also indicates the humanity of Jesus Christ.
Son of David	This indicates Jesus is the promised heir of King David who will reign over the Church, the new Israel, for ever.

When the fullness of time had come, God sent his Son, born of a woman, born a subject of the Law, to redeem the subjects of the Law, so that we could receive adoption as sons.
Galatians 4:4 – 5; *Catechism of the Catholic Church* n. 422

True God and True Man

The divinity and humanity of Jesus Christ were revealed throughout his life on earth. Elizabeth hailed Mary as 'mother of my Lord' and wise men came to worship him at his birth (Mt 2:11). The Gospel of John states that the Word, who is God, became flesh:

> *In the beginning was the Word, and the Word was with God, and the Word was God. He was in the beginning with God; all things were made through him, and without him was not anything made that was made ... And the Word became flesh and dwelt among us, full of grace and truth; we have beheld his glory, glory as of the only Son from the Father.*
>
> Jn 1:1-3, 14

The 'Word made flesh' is the origin of the term 'Incarnation', from the Latin *caro-nis*, meaning 'flesh', and *in*, meaning 'into'. The meaning and implications of the Incarnation are set out in the Creed.

The Nativity by Petrus Christus

The Incarnation in the Creed

JESUS IS TRUE GOD

I believe in one Lord, Jesus Christ, the only Son of God, eternally begotten of the Father, God from God, Light from Light, true God from true God, begotten, not made, one in Being with the Father. Through him all things were made.

He was, is and always will be God with the Father and the Holy Spirit.

He is *begotten not made*, a divine person, not a created person like us. All created things came to be through him.

JESUS IS TRUE MAN

For us men and for our salvation he came down from heaven: by the power of the Holy Spirit he was born of the Virgin Mary, and became man.

He became man, body and soul, participating fully in human life, and remaining incarnate to unite humanity with God forever.

MISTAKES ABOUT THE INCARNATION

☒ **Docetism**	Denies that Jesus has come 'in the flesh', and claims that he only *appears* to be human.
☒ **Arianism**	Denies that Jesus is truly God, and claims he is only a subordinate 'god' or merely a creature.
☒ **Nestorianism**	Denies that Jesus is one person, God the Son, and claims he is two conjoined persons.
☒ **Monophysitism**	Denies that Jesus has a distinct human nature and claims his divinity absorbs his humanity.

The Incarnation and the *Hail Mary*

The prayer *Hail Mary* is based on the words of the Angel Gabriel and Elizabeth to Mary. It includes the title 'Mother of God' because of the Incarnation.

Hail Mary, full of grace, the Lord is with thee. Blessed art thou among women, and blessed is the fruit of thy womb, Jesus. Holy Mary, Mother of God, pray for us sinners now and at the hour of our death. Amen

References

Catechism of the Catholic Church:
ccc. 422-486 (*Compendium* questions 79-104)

Further reading:
SAWARD, J., *Cradle of Redeeming Love*, Ignatius Press,
SCHÖNBORN, CHRISTOPH CARDINAL, *God's Human Face*, Ignatius Press

The Life of Christ

We are witnesses to all that he did.
Acts 10:39

What is the Life of Christ?

The life of Christ is the life that the incarnate Son of God lived upon earth from the time of his conception until his Ascension.

Triumphal Entry by Giotto di Bondone

The principal events of the life of Christ

c. 6 BC	**Conception and birth** His miraculous conception in Nazareth and his birth in Bethlehem
to c. 24 AD	**Hidden life** His thirty years living in Nazareth, known as the carpenter's son
to c. 27 AD	**Public ministry** His three year mission preaching the Kingdom of God, working signs and miracles and establishing his Church
c. 27 AD	**Death, Resurrection, Ascension** His submission to a cruel execution on a cross as a sacrifice for sin; his Resurrection and Ascension into glory

The public ministry of Jesus Christ

JESUS REVEALED HIS IDENTITY

Jesus witnessed to his unique relationship and oneness with 'the Father', referring to himself as the beloved Son (Mt 11:27; Mk 12:6; Lk 20:13). He clearly asserted his own eternal existence and divinity by applying to himself the name of God revealed to Moses, *"Before Abraham was, I AM"* (Jn 8:58, cf. Exod 3:14). He witnessed to his divine power by great nature miracles (Mt 8:26; Mk 6:48), and by forgiving sins, *"My son, your sins are forgiven"* (Mk 2:5).

JESUS EXPLAINED HIS MISSION

Jesus explained that he was to die for the salvation of the world (Jn 12:32) and to share with us the divine life of the Father, Son and Holy Spirit (Mt 28:19). His inaugurating of the Kingdom of God was shown by his victory over evil in forgiving sins, casting out demons and healing the sick (Mk 1:23-27; 5:22-43; Mt 10:7-8).

JESUS TAUGHT HIS NEW DOCTRINE

Jesus taught about the new life of grace through parables and especially the Sermon on the Mount (Mt 5). He showed that the greatest commandment of the law was love of God and neighbour (Mt 22:36-39). Before his death he gave his disciples a new commandment to *"love one another as I have loved you"* (Jn 13:34), a love made possible only by sharing in his own divine love.

JESUS FOUNDED HIS CHURCH

In choosing twelve apostles, Jesus established a visible Church, a new Israel (Mt 10:2; 19:28). He gave authority to Peter and the other apostles to govern and to teach, *"Whatever you bind on earth will be bound in heaven"* (Mt 16:19). He also gave sacramental rites, *"Do this in remembrance of me"* (Lk 22:19). These superseded the ancient Jewish rites, empowering us to be born again in Baptism and to live the new life of grace.

The common timescale of all human history is now measured by the coming of Christ. The words 'before Christ' (BC) refer to the years prior to his birth. The words 'anno Domini' (AD), 'in the year of the Lord', acknowledge his continuing reign.

For we did not follow cleverly devised myths when we made known to you the power and coming of our Lord Jesus Christ, but we were eyewitnesses of his majesty.
2 Peter 1:16

Knowing Jesus Christ

The three senses in which we know Jesus Christ are through reason, faith and personally.

The Calling of Saint Matthew by Caravaggio

Knowing Jesus Christ through reason

We know Jesus Christ though reason, that is, we know of his existence, the world in which he lived, the events of his life and his teaching.

We know these things principally by means of the twenty-seven documents known as the New Testament. These constitute the largest volume of written evidence in the ancient world about any one person. Non-Christian historians of that period also refer to him, in particular Josephus and Tacitus.

> The New Testament documents were all written some twenty to seventy years after the public ministry of Jesus Christ. They were commonly accepted in the early Church as having been written under the authority of the apostles. The four gospels provide mutual corroboration of the events of Jesus' life. While they use a variety of styles, details and arrangements, a single clear personality emerges from the texts.

He who saw it has borne witness, his testimony is true, and he knows that he tells the truth, that you also may believe.

Jn 19:35

Knowing Jesus Christ through faith

We also know Jesus Christ through the gift of faith. This is like an illumination of the mind that God gives us. This gift enables us to recognise and trust in Christ and to accept everything he has revealed.

Faith enables us to know that Jesus Christ is truly:

- God, the second person of the Trinity, *"You are the Christ, the Son of the living God"* (Mt 16:16).
- The 'Lamb of God' (Jn 1:36), the sacrifice that takes away the sins of the world.
- The only way to our salvation, *"I am the way, the truth and the life"* (Jn 14:6).

We can give a human assent to these teachings if we judge Jesus Christ to be trustworthy. Indeed, given the perfection of Jesus' moral character, the depth of his teaching and the evidence of his miracles, his claims have a strong rational credibility. However, it is only with the supernatural gift and assent of faith that we can know Jesus and all that he has revealed with a kind of inner illumination of mind and heart.

No one can say "Jesus is Lord" except by the Holy Spirit.

1 Cor 12:3

Knowing Jesus Christ personally

By personal knowledge, we are enabled to encounter Jesus, not merely as an historical figure to be studied or agreed with, but rather as the living Lord who said *"I am with you always"* (Mt 28:20). This encounter is made possible through prayer, the sacraments and by conforming our lives to the pattern of his life.

The Christian is part of Christ's own mystical body through grace, which means being united spiritually to Christ. In all the sacraments we come to know Jesus intimately. Through the Eucharist, in particular, we receive him, body, blood, soul and divinity. In reading the Scriptures we meet the character of Jesus and are led into conversation with him. In prayer we speak directly to Jesus as a friend and come to an awareness of his presence.

"No longer do I call you servants, for the servant does not know what his master is doing; but I have called you friends, for all that I have heard from my Father I have made known to you."

Jn 15:15

References

Catechism of the Catholic Church:
ccc. 512-570 (*Compendium* questions 105-111)

Further reading:
SHEEN, F., ARCHBISHOP, *The Life of Christ*, Image Books; SHEED, F., *To Know Christ Jesus*, Ignatius Press; REDFORD, J., *Bad, Mad or God? Proving the Divinity of Christ from St. John's Gospel*, St Paul's Publishing

The Paschal Mystery

Behold, the Lamb of God, who takes away the sins of the world!
John 1:29

> The Paschal mystery is the Passion, death and Resurrection of Jesus Christ by which he heals us from sin and enables us to become children of God.

The Passion of Jesus

The Passion of Jesus Christ is his sacrificial suffering and death by crucifixion on mount Calvary.

Jesus told his disciples of these events before they took place. He also made it clear to them that he would suffer freely for the salvation of the world.

> *"The Son of Man will be delivered to the chief priests and scribes, and they will condemn him to death, and deliver him to the Gentiles to be mocked and scourged and crucified, and he will be raised on the third day."* Mt 20:18-19

After his Last Supper, Jesus was arrested in the Garden of Gethsemane outside the walls of Jerusalem. He was tried, found guilty and handed over to Pontius Pilate who ordered him to be crucified. Jesus was then scourged, crowned with thorns and led to the hill of Calvary carrying his own cross. While being crucified, he prayed, *"Father, forgive them; for they know not what they do "* (Lk 23:34). As he died he said, *"It is accomplished "* (Jn 19:30).

What is the atonement?

The word 'atonement' describes Christ's saving action well. It implies both a repayment for our sins (*to atone*) and a reunion of God and humanity (making *at-one*).

> *"You know that you were ransomed from the futile ways inherited from your fathers, not with perishable things such as silver or gold, but with the precious blood of Christ, like that of a lamb without blemish or spot."* 1 Pet 1:18

The atonement is accomplished through a sacrificial petition offered by Christ to God, the divine love of which utterly revokes the offence of all sins and bears the pain and cost of sin in itself. Only a person who was truly divine, human and innocent could make such an effective sacrifice on our behalf.

The Crucifixion by Giotto di Bondone

The atonement and ourselves

WHAT THE ATONEMENT DOES FOR US	
Repays our debt of guilt	*"The Son of Man came ... to serve and to give his life as a ransom "* Mt 20:28.
Gains mercy for us and repeals our punishment	*Upon him was the punishment that made us whole* (Isa 53:5); *"This is my blood ... which is poured out for many for the forgiveness of sins "* (Mt 26:28).
Defeats the claims of the devil over us	*"Now shall the ruler of this world be cast out "* (Jn 12:31); *deliver those ... subject to lifelong bondage ...* (Heb 2:15).
Reconciles us to God	*In Christ God was reconciling the world to himself* (2 Cor 5:19).
Fulfils Scripture and salvation history	*As a plan for the fullness of time, to unite all things in him, things in heaven and things on earth, making peace by the blood of his cross* (Col 1:20).

The atonement also teaches us the seriousness of sin, by the bitterness of its remedy, and manifests the extent of God's love for us, *"God shows his love for us in that while we were yet sinners Christ died for us"* (Rom 5:8). By the atonement, Jesus has also given us the supreme example of sacrificial love, *"Greater love has no man than this, that a man lay down his life for his friends "* (Jn 15:13).

> *The Paschal mystery has two aspects: by his death, Christ liberates us from sin; by his Resurrection, he opens for us the way to a new life.*
> *Catechism of the Catholic Church, n. 654*

The Resurrection of Jesus

The descent to the dead

The soul of Jesus descends to the dead in the period between his death and Resurrection. Scripture refers to him *"preaching to the spirits in prison"* (1 Pet 3:18-20). In other words, he released those just souls who had died before his coming and opened heaven to them.

What is the Resurrection?

The Resurrection is Jesus Christ's bodily rising from the dead after three days in the tomb.

He appeared to Cephas (Peter), then to the twelve. Then he appeared to more than five hundred brethren at one time, most of whom are still alive. 1 Cor 15:4-6

St Peter states that Jesus rose *physically*: "[we] *ate and drank with him after he rose from the dead"* (Acts 10:41), but his glorified body had extraordinary new abilities. He appeared at different times and places at will, and his body, though glorified and transformed in appearance, still bore the wounds of the crucifixion:

"Put your finger here, and see my hands; and put out your hand, and place it in my side; do not be faithless, but believing." Thomas answered him, "My Lord and my God!" Jn 20:28

MISTAKES ABOUT THE RESURRECTION

☒ **A ghostly resurrection**	Denies that Jesus rose in his human body, and claims that only his soul or ghost returned.
☒ **A 'moral' resurrection**	Denies that Jesus lives on, and interprets his Resurrection as a mere continuation of his message.
☒ **A mere revival**	Denies that Jesus' risen body was glorified, and claims that he merely returned to his former condition.
☒ **A failed crucifixion**	Denies that Jesus really died, and claims that he was resuscitated or was part of an elaborate hoax.

If Christ has not been raised, then our preaching is in vain and your faith is in vain. 1 Cor 15:14

The Resurrection by Piero della Francesca

The importance of the Resurrection for us

By his Resurrection, Jesus Christ confirmed:

- that human life does not cease with death;
- the promise of a glorified risen humanity;
- the validity of all he taught and did.

For as in Adam all die, so also in Christ shall all be made alive. But each in his own order: Christ the first fruits, then at his coming those who belong to Christ. 1 Cor 15:22-23

He also gave the disciples the power to forgive sins, the promise of the Holy Spirit, and the great commission to preach the Gospel to all nations.

What is the Ascension?

The Ascension is Jesus' physical departure from his disciples. This event took place after forty days of appearances and teaching following his Resurrection.

Scripture records him *ascending* to heaven, which signifies the *"definitive entrance of Jesus' humanity into God's heavenly domain"* (ccc. 665).

Jesus is now in heaven, where he intercedes and prepares a place for us, and from where he shall come again at the end of time.

References

Catechism of the Catholic Church:
ccc. 571-667 (*Compendium* questions 112-132)

Further reading:
SHEEN, F., ARCHBISHOP, *The Life of Christ*; SHEED, F., *To Know Christ Jesus*; RATZINGER, J. *Behold the pierced one*, Ignatius Press; MORISON F., *Who moved the Stone?*, Faber and Faber

The Trinity

The grace of the Lord Jesus Christ and the love of God and the fellowship of the Holy Spirit be with you all.
2 Corinthians 13:11

eVANGELIUM

The Trinity is the one God in three persons, Father, Son and Holy Spirit.

The Revelation of the Trinity

The revelation of the one God

The existence of the one God has been known to faith and reason throughout history. God chose to reveal himself as one God to the people of Israel, to teach them that he is the creator of all things and the single, true and exclusive object of worship.

Hear, O Israel: The Lord our God is one LORD; and you shall love the LORD your God with all your heart, and with all your soul, and with all your might. Deut 6:4-5

The Old Testament gives glimpses of personal distinctions in God. An example is the use of the plural pronoun 'us' at the creation of human beings.

Then God said, "Let us make man in our image, after our likeness."
Gen 1:26

The revelation of the three persons

In the New Testament, when God the Son becomes man, he openly reveals the persons in God. First the relationship between Father and Son is revealed:

"No one has ever seen God; the only Son, who is in the bosom of the Father, he has made him known." Jn 1:18

He then reveals the relationship of the Father and the Son with the Spirit:

"When the Paraclete comes, whom I shall send to you from the Father, the Spirit of truth who issues from the Father, he will be my witness." Jn 15:26 NJB

All Christian life begins with Baptism in the name of the three divine persons, following Jesus' command:

"Make disciples of all nations; baptise them in the name of the Father and of the Son and of the Holy Spirit." Mt 28:19-20 NJB

The three divine persons are the One Triune God.

The Holy Trinity with Mary Magdalene, St John the Baptist and Tobias and the Angel by Alessandro Botticelli

The Trinity in Creed and worship

The Trinity is the central theme of the Apostles' Creed, a summary of Christian belief from the early Church that is also an important liturgical prayer.

GOD THE FATHER

I believe in God, the Father Almighty, Creator of heaven and earth.

GOD THE SON

I believe in Jesus Christ, his only son, our Lord. He was conceived by the power of the Holy Spirit and born of the Virgin Mary. He suffered under Pontius Pilate, was crucified, died and was buried. He descended into hell. On the third day he rose again. He ascended into heaven and is seated at the right hand of the Father. He will come again to judge the living and the dead.

GOD THE HOLY SPIRIT

I believe in the Holy Spirit, the holy catholic Church the communion of saints, the forgiveness of sins, the resurrection of the body, and life everlasting. Amen.

The mystery of the Most Holy Trinity is the central mystery of the Christian faith and of Christian life.

Catechism of the Catholic Church, n. 261

What is the Trinity?

One substance, three persons

God alone reveals the Trinity since it is the mystery of his very being. Human reason can know that there *is* a God; we cannot know God as he knows himself except from what God has revealed.

The fact that Jesus Christ reveals the relationship of Father, Son and Holy Spirit, tells us that these are distinct divine persons. Each divine person can properly say 'I', as when Jesus says "*I and the Father are One*" (Jn 10:30). Jesus also uses a personal pronoun (translated 'he') of the Holy Spirit when he says, "*the Counsellor, the Holy Spirit, whom the Father will send in my name, he will teach you all things*" (Jn 14:26; cf. 15:26; 16:13-15).

Nevertheless, the relations within the Trinity differ from those among human persons. Our relationships are changeable, and are established from person to person over time. By contrast, the relations of the divine persons are the very being or 'substance' of God. They are eternal and unchanging. This unity of substance and distinction of persons is expressed in the Trinitarian formula of St Gregory Nazianzus, which Pope St Damasus I affirmed:

The Trinity is one substance, three persons.

Mistaken beliefs about the Trinity

The challenge of speaking about the Trinity leads to frequent mistakes. These deny one aspect or another of the 'one substance, three persons' of the Trinity.

MISTAKES ABOUT THE TRINITY	
☒ **Modalism**	Denies that the Father, Son and Spirit are three persons, and sees them as mere appearances, or masks, of one person.
☒ **Tri-theism**	Denies that there is one God, and claims that the Father, Son and Spirit are three gods.
☒ **Subordinationism**	Denies that the Son and the Spirit are equal in divinity to the Father, claiming that they are subordinate to him.

The Trinity by Andrei Rublev

The Trinity and our friendship with God

God does not want us to relate to him merely as creatures to their Creator. The remarkable invitation that God has given to us is to enjoy intimate friendship with him by sharing his divine life. This is the precise reason why God has revealed the Trinity to us, so that we may come to know and love him as he knows and loves himself. This is why:

- All Christian belief is Trinitarian (for example, the Creed).

- All sacraments are Trinitarian (for example, Baptism is in the name of the Trinity).

- All Christian life is directed towards union with the Trinity (for example, the virtue of charity).

- All Christian prayer is Trinitarian (for example, blessings and the Sign of the Cross).

As you are sons, God has sent into our hearts the Spirit of his Son crying, "Abba, Father." Gal 4:6 NJB

References

Catechism of the Catholic Church:
ccc. 199-267; 687-747 (*Compendium* questions 33-50; 136-146)

Further reading:
ST AUGUSTINE, *The Trinity*, trans. Edmund Hill, New City Press; HAHN, S., *First Comes Love*, DLT; EMERY, G., *Trinity in Aquinas*, Ave Maria; KELLY, J. N. D., *Early Christian Doctrines*, Mowbray

The Church

Christ is the head of the Church, his body, and is himself its Saviour.
Ephesians 5:23

*e*VANGELIUM

What is the Church?

> The Church is the mystical body of Christ, established by God on earth to gather humanity to divine life in heaven.

God desires all the faithful to be a single family, united to him and to one another in one 'mystical body'. This assembly is the Church, the body of Christ, which God has established as the *"instrument for the salvation of all"* (*Lumen Gentium* 9§2, ccc. 776).

The Church in the Creed

THE CHARACTERISTICS OF THE CHURCH

'We believe in One, Holy, Catholic and Apostolic Church'

ONE Jn 11:52	She is one because she has one founder, God. She is also one because her members are united in one faith, sharing the same sacraments under one head, Christ, and the Pope, his vicar on earth.
HOLY Eph 5:25-27	She is holy because she is founded by God, and because her members are the baptised. Through her ministry sinners receive Christ's forgiveness and become holy.
CATHOLIC Rev 7:9	She is Catholic, which means 'universal', because she is for all races and nations in all ages. All salvation comes through her.
APOSTOLIC Acts 15:1-33	She is apostolic because her faith and practices have come to her from the apostles. Her leaders, the bishops, are successors of the apostles. She is also apostolic in that she is 'sent out' to preach the Gospel to all creation.

The foundation of the Church by Christ

Christ handing the keys to St Peter by Pietro Perugino

Jesus Christ established a group of followers under twelve leaders he called 'Apostles'. He gave one of them, Simon Peter, overall authority.

> *"You are Peter, and on this rock I will build my church, and the powers of death shall not prevail against it. I will give you the keys of the kingdom of heaven, and whatever you bind on earth shall be bound in heaven, and whatever you loose on earth shall be loosed in heaven."* Mt 16:18-19

He gave his disciples his teaching to pass on to all peoples under the direction of the Holy Spirit who came at Pentecost. This teaching is found in Scripture and Tradition, and is interpreted by the Church with the authority of Christ.

He also established the sacraments to enable his saving power to be present through the ministry of the Church. *"Do this in remembrance of me"* (Lk 22:19).

MISTAKES ABOUT THE CHURCH

☒ **An invisible church**	The denial that Christ founded a visible institution; the claim that the present structures of Catholic leadership are a human invention.
☒ **A church without a Pope**	The denial of the true hierarchical structure of the Church with bishops united to, and under the authority of, the Pope, the successor of Peter.

> *I am writing these instructions to you so that ... you may know how one ought to behave in the household of God, which is the church of the living God, the pillar and bulwark of the truth.*
> 1 Timothy 3:14-15

Where is the Church?

The Church on earth

St Paul calls the Church the 'body of Christ' (Eph 1:22-23). As a *body*, she has an ordered structure and a visible unity. As *Christ's* body, she is both a divine and human reality (ccc. 771).

The principal visible elements of this structure are the bishop of Rome (Pope), all the bishops of the world in communion with him, their priests and deacons, those in religious life and the lay faithful.

The institution of the Church extends across all nations. The whole world is divided up into dioceses under the authority of bishops. Dioceses are in turn divided into parishes under the direction of priests.

The Church also includes institutes of consecrated life following particular vocational paths. These include religious orders such as the Benedictines, Dominicans, Franciscans and Jesuits. There are also secular institutes, societies of apostolic life and many lay associations. The majority of the Church's members are lay people whose special calling is to personal holiness and the evangelisation and sanctification of the societies in which they live.

> Baptism is the means of entry into the Catholic Church, but not all the baptised remain fully united with her. These include Protestant and Orthodox Christians. The Catholic Church believes that her essential structures and teachings are divinely established. She recognises, however, all that is good and true in other Christian communions, for instance, the validity of all Orthodox sacraments. She is committed to the prayer and work for Christian unity which is called *ecumenism*.

The Church in purgatory

Since those who have died and are in purgatory are also part of the Church, the Church is also found in purgatory. This is why we in the Church on earth offer prayers and sacrifices for the purification and reparation of the holy souls of the dead.

> *Therefore he made atonement for the dead, that they might be delivered from their sin.* 2 Macc 12:45

The Church in heaven

The goal of the Church is to be united with God in the glory of heaven. Just as Christians on earth comprise a community, those in heaven also form a community. This is the Church in glory, which the Apostles' Creed calls 'the communion of saints'.

The San Marco altarpiece by Fra Angelico

> The word *saint* means 'holy one', a title of honour given to those who are now in the glory of heaven. Although most saints are unknown to us, the Church has recognised that certain men and women, from all ages and states of life, are definitely now in heaven. Some examples are the *apostles* St Peter and St John; the *martyrs* St Agnes and St Thomas More; the *virgins* St Clare and St Edith Stein; and the *pastors* St John Vianney and St Philip Neri. The Church honours exemplary teachers, such as St Thomas Aquinas and St Teresa of Avila, with the title *doctor of the Church*.

We in the Church on earth are joined in prayer with the saints in heaven. We therefore honour them and pray for their intercession in our earthly pilgrimage.

In Scripture, the Church in glory is described as the 'bride of Christ' and the 'new Jerusalem'.

> *I saw a new heaven and a new earth ... And I saw the holy city, the new Jerusalem, coming down out of heaven from God, prepared as a bride adorned for her husband.* Rev 21:1-2

References

Catechism of the Catholic Church:
ccc. 748-962 (*Compendium* questions 147-195)

Further reading:
RAY, S., *Upon this Rock*, Ignatius Press; RATZINGER, J., *Called to Communion*, Ignatius Press; CHARLES J., *The Theology of the Church*, Ignatius Press

Scripture and Tradition

The word of God is living and active, sharper than any two-edged sword.

Hebrews 4:12

Scripture and Tradition together constitute the single deposit of revealed truth given by God to the Church and infallibly taught by the Magisterium.

What is Scripture?

Scripture is the single collection of 73 books called the Bible. It is the entire content of God's inspired written truth, revealing himself and his saving plan.

Given its importance for salvation, God, through the inspiration of the Holy Spirit, has guaranteed that the Bible records faithfully and without error, everything that he wanted written and no more (cf. *Dei Verbum* 11).

Saint Matthew writing his Gospel by Caravaggio

What is Tradition?

Tradition is what is revealed by God and handed on by the apostles, including those things not explicitly recorded in Scripture. 'Tradition' comes from the Latin *tradere*, which means 'to hand on'. The disciples taught before they wrote, and this oral teaching remained authoritative alongside written Scripture.

Hold to the traditions which you were taught by us, either by word of mouth or by letter. 2 Thess 2:15

Tradition expresses that breadth of divine teaching which cannot be exhaustively communicated in any one written form, as the apostle John states:

There are also many other things which Jesus did; were every one of them to be written, I suppose that the world itself could not contain the books that would be written. Jn 21:25

Some truths of Tradition have subsequently been given dogmatic definition by the 'Magisterium'. Examples are the number of the sacraments and Mary's Assumption. The definition of the books of Scripture is itself the fruit of Tradition.

Other manifestations of Tradition can be found in the liturgy, art and music of the Church.

What is the Magisterium?

The Magisterium is the teaching office of the Church exercised by the Pope, the successor of Peter, and the bishops in union with him. With the authority of Jesus Christ (Jn 16:13; Mt 16:19) the Magisterium teaches infallibly the revealed truth which Scripture and Tradition communicate.

I would not believe in the Gospel, had not the authority of the Catholic Church already moved me.

St Augustine, *Contra Epistolam Manichaei* 5, 6 (ccc. 119)

The principal teachings of the Magisterium are the dogmatic decrees of the papacy, the Creeds and the other doctrines of the twenty-one Ecumenical Councils since the time of the apostles.

In the supreme wise arrangement of God, Sacred Tradition, Sacred Scripture and the Magisterium of the Church are so connected and associated that one of them cannot stand without the others.

Dei Verbum, n. 10, cited in the *Catechism of the Catholic Church* n. 95

OLD TESTAMENT	NEW TESTAMENT

46 books				27 books				
PENTATEUCH	**FORMER PROPHETS**	**LATER PROPHETS**	**WRITINGS**	**GOSPELS**	**ACTS**	**PAULINE WORKS**	**CATHOLIC LETTERS**	**REVEL-ATION**
Genesis	Joshua	Isaiah	Psalms	Matthew	Acts of	Romans	James	Revelation
Exodus	Judges	Jeremiah	Proverbs	Mark	the	Galatians	I, II Peter	*or*
Numbers	[Ruth]	Ezekiel	Chronicles	Luke	Apostles	Ephesians	I-III John	Apocalypse
Leviticus	I, II Samuel	Daniel	Job	John		Titus	Jude	
Deuteronomy	I, II Kings	*and others*	*and others*			*and others*		

Most of these books were written in HEBREW. Here is a short example:	All these books were written in GREEK. Here is a short example:
אֶהְיֶה אֲשֶׁר אֶהְיֶה	Ἐν ἀρχῇ ἦν ὁ λόγος
"I AM who AM" (Ex 3:14).	*"In the beginning was the Word"* (Jn 1:1).

These books were written over the period c. 1200 – c. 100 BC	These books were written over the period c. 50 – c. 100 AD
BEFORE ←	→ **AFTER**
the birth of Jesus Christ	**the death and Resurrection of Christ**

How do I navigate Scripture?

Any text in the Bible, such as **Mt 27:1-2**, can be found from:

- the title of the book: **Mt** (Matthew)
- the chapter number: **27**
- the verses: **2**

The book titles, their abbreviations and page numbers can be found at the beginning of any Bible.

Catholic and Protestant Bibles have slightly different structures. From early Tradition, and with her infallible authority, the Catholic Church accepts among the inspired books of the Old Testament: Tobit, Judith, 1 and 2 Maccabees, the Wisdom of Solomon, Sirach (Ecclesiasticus), Baruch and some additional parts of Daniel and Esther (ccc. 120). Protestant traditions set aside these books from the Old Testament, calling them 'apocrypha'.

75 Then Peter remembered what Jesus had said: "Before the cock crows, you will deny me three times." And he went out and wept bitterly.

Jesus Brought Before Pilate

27 When morning came, all the chief priests and the elders of the people conferred together against Jesus in order to bring about his death **2** They bound him, led him away, and handed him over to Pilate the governor.

An example of the chapter and verse numbers of a Biblical text, Mt 27:2

AUTHENTIC READING OF SCRIPTURE

Read as one – The Bible must be read as a unified work in which God has chosen to reveal himself. Although the Bible is made up of many diverse texts from different times and cultures, it reveals a single story of God's providence and salvation. The Old Testament points towards its own fulfilment in the New; the meaning of the New Testament is manifested by the Old.

Read within the Tradition – God has entrusted the whole of Scripture to the Church. It is only by the Church's authority that the Bible's 73 books are recognised as the unified word of God. Only the Church has the right and capability of authoritatively expounding Scripture. Profound insight into Scripture is found in the writings of the saints, fathers and doctors of the Church.

Read in the literal sense – The literal sense is the primary and direct sense of Scripture which God intends to convey through human agency. It is the meaning the writer intends, the interpretation of which is aided by the study of history and context. A literal reading does not mean a *literalistic* reading of texts intended as metaphors or parables. The literal sense also includes the making of cross-references among Biblical books.

Read in the spiritual sense – In the spiritual sense of Scripture God has ensured that the realities mentioned in the text can also point to *other* realities. *Allegory* often links something mentioned in Scripture, especially in the Old Testament, to Christ or to the Church. *Tropology* (the moral sense) links something described in Scripture to the living of the Christian life of grace. *Anagogy* links the realities mentioned in Scripture to those of heaven.

References

Catechism of the Catholic Church:
ccc. 74-141 (*Compendium* questions 6-24)

Further reading:
BAKER, K., *Inside the Bible*, Ignatius Press; HAHN, S., *Scripture Matters*, Emmaus Road; HAHN, S., MITCH, C., *Ignatius Study Bible Series*, Ignatius Press; MADRID, P., *Why is that in Tradition?*, Our Sunday Visitor

Mary and the Four Last Things

A great sign appeared in heaven: a woman, robed with the sun, standing on the moon, and on her head a crown of twelve stars. Revelation 12:1

*e*VANGELIUM

Mary, the Mother of Jesus

Mary was conceived immaculate. As a virgin, she became Mother of God by bearing Jesus Christ. She was without sin, was assumed body and soul into heaven, and is the Mother of the Church.

Why is she called 'Mother of God'?

Mary is called 'Mother of God' because she became the mother of Jesus Christ, true God and true man.

Elizabeth called Mary 'the mother of my Lord' (Lk 1:43) and the Council of Ephesus (431) declared Mary to be 'Mother of God' and not only of Christ's humanity. This title, part of the *Hail Mary*, recognises that Jesus is a single person, God and man.

Why is she called the 'Virgin Mary'?

Mary has this title because she was and remained a virgin before, during and after Jesus' birth.

Mary's question to Gabriel, "*How can this be, since I am a virgin?*" (Lk 1:34), reveals her virginal commitment. The angel's response, "*The Holy Spirit will come upon you and the power of the most High will overshadow you*" (Lk 1:34) shows that this proposed conception would be miraculous and preserving of Mary's dedication to a virginal life. Mary's continued virginity is also fitting for the chosen spouse of the Holy Spirit. As Mother of the Church, Mary bears many spiritual children.

What is the Immaculate Conception?

Mary was conceived immaculate and spared from Original Sin and its effects from her beginning.

In Scripture Mary is 'blessed among women' (Lk 1:42), and 'full of grace' (cf. Lk 1:28). Pope Pius IX officially defined the dogma of the Immaculate Conception in 1854. Mary appeared to St Bernadette at Lourdes in 1858 and declared "*I am the Immaculate Conception.*"

The Coronation of the Virgin by Enguerrand Quarton

What is her Assumption?

The Assumption teaches that Mary was taken body and soul into heaven at the end of her earthly life.

Death is a punishment for sin (Gen 3). One without sin should not experience the grave, since "*You will not let your holy one see decay*" (Acts 2:27). As Mary shared closely in the saving death of Christ, she is first to share his Resurrection. She is therefore in heaven, body and soul, "*a woman clothed with the sun, with the moon under her feet, and on her head a crown of twelve stars*" (Rev 12:1). Her Assumption also points to our own resurrection.

The importance of Mary for us

In Mary we see our human nature gloriously restored and raised to heaven. As our mother in Christ, she also protects and intercedes for us all.

Mary became the Mother of the Church when Christ made her mother of the beloved disciple, representing all Christians, "*Behold, your mother!*" (Jn 19:27). As the first Eve is the mother of all the living; so Mary is the 'Second Eve', the mother of all the redeemed. "*All generations will call me blessed*" (Lk 1:28).

The Mother of Jesus, in the glory which she possesses in body and soul in heaven, is the image and beginning of the Church as it is to be perfected in the world to come.

Lumen Gentium n. 68 cited in the *Catechism of the Catholic Church* n. 972

The Four Last Things

The Four Last Things are the two *inevitable* and two *possible* realities that we face at the end of our earthly lives.

DEATH

Human beings die only once, after which comes judgment.

Heb 9:27

Death is the cessation of our present earthly lives, the moment of separation of our souls and bodies. Once dead, we cease to choose between good and evil: death irrevocably fixes our state for eternity. Although death came to us because of sin, not God's will, God has removed its terror for us and made it the path to eternal life.

We should remain in God's friendship and live each day as if it were our last. We should also ask God for the grace of a good and holy death.

JUDGMENT

First, there is a particular and unchangeable judgment which follows immediately upon our deaths. Second, as the Creed affirms, there is a final and universal reckoning at the end of time when Christ *"will come again"*. At this Second Coming he will *"judge the living"*, those still alive, *"and the dead"*, united physically with their resurrected bodies.

They will give account to him who is ready to judge the living and the dead.

1 Pet 4:5

As we are to be judged by God, we should ask for his mercy and help to put our lives in order, examine our consciences regularly and practise Confession.

HELL

Depart from me, you cursed, into the eternal fire prepared for the devil and his angels.

Mt 25:41

Hell is the eternal loss of the vision of God, and the place of punishment of damned souls, the devil and his angels. It is the choice of evil and lack of repentance before the end of our earthly lives that leads to our damnation. After the Fall, hell would have been the just end of the human race. God in his great love, however, has offered us salvation through the blood of Jesus Christ.

We should ask God to save us from the 'fires of hell' (cf. Mt 18:9; Rev 20:14) as he himself desires (1 Tim 2:4). We also have a duty to warn others, just as Jesus warned us, of the reality of hell and the need to repent and follow him in our lives.

HEAVEN

Heaven is our eternal home where God gives us the vision of his face and shares his divine life with us. Scripture describes heaven as a city or kingdom where the saints enjoy the perfected creation and the reward they deserve. Those who die in God's grace either go straight to heaven or first enter *purgatory*, a place of purification for sins and for reparation.

Come, O blessed of my Father, inherit the kingdom prepared for you from the foundation of the world

Mt 25:34

We can truly hope for heaven since it is God's desire for us. We should ask him to prepare us for heaven even if we face sufferings on the way. It is good to make the saints our companions through prayer and to pray for the holy souls in purgatory (cf. 2 Macc 12:44).

Death, judgment, hell and heaven: details from *The Seven Deadly Sins* by Hieronymous Bosch

References

Catechism of the Catholic Church:
ccc. 964-975; 988-1060 (*Compendium* questions 94-100, 133-135, 196-199; 202-216)

Further reading:
HAHN, S., *Hail, Holy Queen: The Mother of God in the Word of God*, DLT; SHEEN, F. J., *The World's First Love*, Ignatius Press. LAGRANGE, G., *Life Everlasting*, Tan Books; MARTIN, R., *The Last Things*, Ignatius Press

Liturgy and Sacraments

True worshippers will worship the Father in spirit and truth.

John 4:13

*e*VANGELIUM

What is the Sacred Liturgy?

The sacred liturgy is the true worship of God, enacted by Jesus Christ and his body, the Church, through the power of the Holy Spirit. It is a shared 'public work' (*leitourgia*) with ceremonies, rites and formulas established by Scripture and Tradition.

Why does the Church have liturgy?

The Church has liturgy in obedience to God. The sacramental rites of the New Testament fulfil and replace the Old Testament rituals. This change is most clearly expressed by Christ's command at Passover, *"Do this in remembrance of me"* (Lk 22:19).

As the true worship of God, it is also clear that the liturgy of the Church should follow the ceremonies, rites and formulas established by Scripture and Tradition where the will of God is revealed.

As we are physical and social beings, it is fitting that the liturgy that God has given to us be public and engage all our senses. Liturgy therefore involves common prayers, visual signs, symbolic actions, sacred music and the proclamation of Scripture.

The Baptism of Christ by Piero della Francesca

When is liturgy celebrated?

Liturgy follows set times and seasons, the most important being when the Church celebrates the Resurrection of Jesus on Sunday and at Easter.

Advent and Christmas	Advent is the four-week period when we prepare for the coming of Jesus Christ at Christmas and for his final coming at the end of time.
Lent and Easter	Lent is the forty-day period of prayer, fasting and almsgiving that follows the pattern of Jesus' own preparation in the wilderness for his mission. Holy week and Easter are when we celebrate his redemptive death and Resurrection.
Ordinary time	Ordinary time covers the rest of the Liturgical Year. Although this period is called 'ordinary', it still includes some special solemnities and feasts.

THE LITURGIES OF THE CHURCH	
The Eucharist and the other sacraments	All these are led by sacred ministers, usually priests, and consist of official prayers, Scripture and sacramental actions.
The Divine Office	These are the prayers that priests, religious and many lay people pray several times each day. They consist mainly of the psalms.
Other rites	These include the *Rite of Christian Initiation for Adults* (RCIA), for reception into the Catholic Church, Benediction and Funeral rites.

The Liturgy is the work of the whole Christ, Head and Body. Our High Priest celebrates it unceasingly in the the heavenly liturgy, with the holy Mother of God, the apostles, all the saints and the multitude of those who have already entered the Kingdom.

Catechism of the Catholic Church n. 1187

What are the Sacraments?

Sacraments are signs established by Christ that cause what they signify. They heal us from sin and plant, nourish or restore the life of grace in us.

Why are sacraments important?

The sacraments are important because they make the power of the Paschal mystery of Jesus Christ present to us for the sake of our salvation. By these seven channels of grace, God makes us his adopted children and increases his life of grace within us.

The Seven Sacraments touch all the stages and all the important moments of Christian life: they give birth and increase, healing and mission to the Christian's life of Faith. There is thus a certain resemblance between the stages of natural life and the stages of the spiritual life. ccc. 1210

What is essential to the sacraments?

Every sacrament has a minister who performs certain actions prescribed by Christ and his Church.

Sacraments are not, however, magic formulas; they require faith and consent (the parents give this in the special case of infant Baptism). It is only when all their conditions are fulfilled that the sacraments bring about their intended spiritual effects.

The Communion of the Apostles by Fra Angelico

What are the effects of the sacraments?

By God's will, the sacraments bring about his divine action. They *cause* what they signify and are not merely signs or symbols of his work. There are seven sacraments with diverse actions and effects.

SACRAMENT	THE LITURGICAL CELEBRATION	THE EFFECTS
Baptism	The minister pours water over the head of the candidate (or immerses him or her) and says, "[Name] *I baptise you in the name of the Father, and of the Son, and of the Holy Spirit.*"	The forgiveness of sins, the new life of grace and membership of the Church
Confirmation	The bishop (or priest) anoints a person's forehead with chrism and says, "*Be sealed with the gift of the Holy Spirit.*"	The sealing with the Holy Spirit for the mature Christian life
Eucharist	The priest consecrates bread and wine, saying, "*This is my body which will be given up for you ....; this is the cup of my blood.*"	Calvary re-presented; the Real Presence; spiritual food
Confession	The penitent confesses sins with sorrow and repentance. The priest gives absolution, "*I absolve you from your sins...*"	The forgiveness of sins and restoration of grace
Anointing	The priest anoints the sick person's forehead and hands with oil, praying the prescribed words.	The forgiveness of sins, spiritual strength and healing
Holy Orders	The bishop lays his hands on the head of the candidate and then says the prayer of consecration for ordination.	The ordination of a minister to act in the person of Christ
Matrimony	The spouses express their consent to one another following the prescribed canonical form, usually before a priest.	The union of the spouses as Christ is united to the Church

References

Catechism of the Catholic Church:
ccc. 1066-1211 (*Compendium* questions 218-250)

Further reading:
HAHN, S., *Swear to God*, DLT, STRAVINSKAS, P., *Understanding the Sacraments*, Ignatius Press;
RATZINGER, J., *The Spirit of the Liturgy*, Ignatius Press; NICHOLS, A. O.P, *Looking at Liturgy*, Ignatius Press

Baptism and Confirmation

You received the Spirit of adoption, enabling us to cry out, "Abba, Father!"
Romans 8:15

*e*VANGELIUM

What is Baptism?

Baptism is the sacrament by which we become Christians. It frees us from Original Sin, makes us children of God and members of the Church.

Why is Baptism important?

Baptism is of the greatest importance for us because it is the ordinary way of salvation for every human being (ccc. 1257). It is the gateway to all the other sacraments and the whole Christian life.

Jesus commanded:

"Go and make disciples of all nations, baptising them in the name of the Father and of the Son and of the Holy Spirit, and teaching them to obey everything I have commanded you."
Mt 28:19-20

St Ambrose linked Baptism to Christ's cross and Resurrection

"See where Baptism comes from, if not from the cross of Christ, from His death. There is the whole mystery: He died for you. In Him you are redeemed, in Him you are saved." ccc. 1225

The Baptism of St Augustine by St Ambrose
by Benito Gozzoli

What happens to us through Baptism?

The water used in Baptism symbolises both washing and new life. The effects of Baptism are:

• The washing away of all sins, particularly the state of Original Sin inherited from our first parents.

• A new life as children of God, members of the Church and temples of the Holy Spirit.

How do we prepare for Baptism?

An adult prepares for Baptism by becoming a *catechumen*, that is, someone who is being catechised (educated) in the Christian Faith. In the Church today there is a formal process and rite for this called the *Rite of Christian Initiation for Adults* (RCIA). This rite prepares an individual or group to receive Baptism, often celebrated at the Easter Vigil.

HOW BAPTISM TAKES PLACE

Who receives Baptism?	Anyone not already baptised can receive Baptism. They must have a belief in the Christian Faith inspired by God.
	Following early Church practice, the Church also baptises the children of Christian parents who make an act of faith and commitment on their child's behalf. New born babies should be baptised as soon as possible.
Who baptises?	A bishop, priest or deacon normally baptises. In cases of necessity (such as danger of death) any person can baptise if they intend to do what the Church does in Baptism. They must use water and the Trinitarian formula.
How is Baptism conferred?	Baptism is conferred by immersion in water, as in the early Church, or by pouring water over the head, together with the proper form of words,
	"[The person's name] **I baptise you in the name of the Father, and of the Son, and of the Holy Spirit."**
	Baptism normally takes place at a font in a church. The baptised person is anointed with the oil of chrism to share in the royal, prophetic and priestly dignity of Christ. A white garment and candle signify freedom from sin and the light of Resurrection.

You were buried with him (Jesus Christ) in baptism, in which you were also raised with him through faith in the working of God, who raised him from the dead.
Colossians 2:12

23

What is Confirmation?

Confirmation completes the Christian initiation begun in Baptism, making us spiritually adult by means of a permanent 'seal' upon our souls.

In this sacrament the Holy Spirit also gives us seven gifts that enable us to see and act well spiritually. These gifts empower us to publicly proclaim the Gospel and to defend the faith against opposition.

Why is Confirmation important?

Confirmation is important because it equips us for living the Christian life in the world, helping us to attain salvation for ourselves and others.

Confirmation and Pentecost

Confirmation perpetuates in the Church the grace of Pentecost, the day when the disciples received the Holy Spirit to preach the gospel (ccc. 1288).

Pentecost by Duccio di Buoninsegna

When the day of Pentecost had come, they were all together in one place. And suddenly from heaven there came a sound like the rush of a violent wind, and it filled the entire house where they were sitting. Divided tongues, as of fire, appeared among them, and a tongue rested on each of them. All of them were filled with the Holy Spirit and began to speak in other languages, as the Spirit gave them ability. Acts 2:1-4

THE SEVEN GIFTS OF THE HOLY SPIRIT

Gifts for seeing in personal union with God

Wisdom	An illumination of the mind, enabling a grasp of the ultimate realities of God and divine things.
Understanding	To see the truth, meaning and implications of what God has revealed (for example, in Scripture).
Knowledge	To see created things in their right relation to God (for example, family life in God's service).

Gifts for acting in personal union with God

Counsel	To perceive the actions we must do in particular situations.
Fortitude (Courage)	To have strength and confidence to accomplish difficult actions.
Piety (Devotion)	To have a familial respect for God, other persons and holy things.
Fear of the Lord (Awe)	To have a holy fear of offending God because of our love of God.

How do we receive Confirmation?

Confirmation is normally given by a bishop to older children or young adults as they begin to take on their full Christian responsibilities.

The rite of Confirmation has the following structure:

- Those about to receive Confirmation renew their baptismal promises.

- The bishop prays over the candidates for the coming of the Holy Spirit.

- The bishop anoints the forehead of each with holy oil (chrism), while praying the words, **"Be sealed with the gift of the Holy Spirit."**

It is God who establishes us with you in Christ, and has commissioned us; he has put his seal upon us and given us his Spirit in our hearts as a guarantee. 2 Cor 1:21-22

References

Catechism of the Catholic Church:
ccc. 1213-1284; 1285-1321 (*Compendium* questions 251-270)

Further reading:
EUSTOCHIUM, SR. *Baptism*, CTS; DAVID, M., *Confirmation*, CTS; YARNOLD, E., *The Awe-Inspiring Rites of Initiation: The Origins of RCIA*, T&T Clarke; PERQUIN, B., *Abba Father*, Scepter; KEATING, D., *Deification and Grace*, Sapientia

The Eucharist

Christ our Passover is sacrificed for us: therefore let us keep the feast.
1 Corinthians 5:7-8 KJV

The Eucharist is a sacrifice, a presence and a food.

- **Sacrifice**. It makes present Jesus Christ's sacrifice on Calvary for our salvation.

- **Presence**. It is Jesus Christ himself under the appearances of bread and wine.

- **Food**. It is the nourishment of our souls by which we share in God's own life.

The Eucharist as Sacrifice

The Eucharist is a sacrament established by Christ to nourish the life of grace in us. Uniquely among the sacraments, however, the Eucharist is also a *sacrifice*, the sacrifice of Christ himself.

Sacrifices offer something up to God to honour him, to thank him, to gain communion with him and to make expiation for sin. The Eucharistic sacrifice of Christ achieves all of these perfectly.

Sacrifices in the Old Testament

Both unbloody and bloody kinds of sacrifice were prominent in the Old Testament. Sacrifices without blood included Melchizedech's offering of bread and wine and the yearly offering of the first-fruits of the harvest. The pre-eminent blood sacrifice was the sacrifice of Passover. Shedding the blood of the Paschal lamb and eating its flesh marked the 'passing over' from sin and death to freedom and life.

These sacrifices were commanded by God as provisional and prophetic, offsetting some of the effects of sin. However, these imperfect sacrifices of fallen humanity could never achieve our redemption or unite us to God in familial communion.

For since the law has but a shadow of the good things to come instead of the true form of these realities, it can never, by the same sacrifices which are continually offered year after year, make perfect those who draw near.   Heb 10:1

The Eucharistic sacrifice of Christ

The Eucharistic sacrifice of Jesus renders perfect thanksgiving to God and gains mercy for the whole world. 'Eucharist' originally meant 'thanksgiving'.

When Jesus began his mission, John the Baptist declared him to be "*the Lamb of God, who takes away the sin of the world*" (Jn 1:29). By these words John indicated that Jesus is the *perfect sacrifice* prefigured by the Old Testament sacrifices.

The Seven Sacraments (centrepiece) by Rogier van der Weyden

Jesus confirmed that he would offer his flesh for the life of the world (Jn 6:51). At the feast of Passover, he took bread and wine and offered up his imminent death for our salvation.

"*Take this, all of you, and eat it: this is my body which will be given up for you.*"

"*Take this, all of you, and drink from it: this is the cup of my blood, the blood of the new and everlasting covenant. It will be shed for you and for all so that sins may be forgiven.*"

Jesus added, "*Do this in memory of me.*" Therefore the Church, through her priests, continues to offer the same Eucharistic sacrifice. Christ's offering on Calvary and its salvific effects are thereby made present to all ages until the end of time.

This Eucharistic sacrifice is called the Mass. It is the centre of the Church's worship, "*the source and summit of the Christian life*" (*Lumen Gentium* n. 11).

For as often as you eat this bread and drink the cup, you proclaim the Lord's death until he comes. Whoever, therefore, eats the bread or drinks the cup of the Lord in an unworthy manner will be guilty of profaning the body and blood of the Lord.
1 Corinthians 11:26 – 27

The Eucharist as Presence

The Institution of the Eucharist by Joos van Wassenhover

Is Jesus really present in the Eucharist?

Jesus promised to give food from heaven that would be his flesh and blood (Jn 6:51-56). He fulfilled this promise at the Last Supper, when he took the bread and said explicitly *"this is my body"* and when he took the wine and said *"this is the cup of my blood."*

This gift is also made present to us today. When the priest speaks the words of consecration in the Mass, the bread and wine truly become the body and blood of Jesus Christ. The Church calls this change 'transubstantiation' because the substance of bread and wine are really changed, becoming the substance of Jesus Christ himself. For this reason, uniquely of all things present to our senses in this world, we worship the Eucharist as God.

Jesus said before his Ascension to the Father: *"I am with you always; yes, to the end of time"* (Mt 28:20). This promise is fulfilled in the real presence of the Eucharist in the tabernacle of every Catholic church. We therefore honour him by genuflecting, kneeling and praying before the tabernacle. Sometimes the Eucharistic host is placed in a monstrance so that we can see the host and offer him adoration.

The Eucharist as Food

Following Jesus' command *"Take this, all of you, and eat it ... Take this...and drink from it"*, the Eucharist has always been celebrated as a sacred meal.

When Christ publicly declared that all must eat his flesh and drink his blood, many were shocked (Jn 6:60). These actions are fitting, though, because of what a spiritual and sacred meal implies:

- **Union**. By consuming his life we become like him, and he dwells within us. For this reason the Eucharist is also called *Holy Communion*. As a meal, it also expresses intimacy with Christ and unity with the whole Church (1 Cor 10:17).

- **Strength**. By consuming divine food, we gain nourishment in the divine life that Christ has shared with us. The form of bread under which it appears is a sign that the Eucharist gives us strength for the spiritual journey through life, and at the approach of death.

- **Promise**. By receiving the risen Jesus, we also receive in the Eucharist the power of his Resurrection within us. As he promised, *"He who eats my flesh and drinks my blood has eternal life, and I will raise him up at the last day"* (Jn 6:56 and 6:40).

The Mystic Lamb (Ghent Altarpiece) by Jan van Eyck

The Mass as a sacred banquet on earth is also our sharing in something far greater in heaven. Scripture refers to a heavenly wedding feast, *"Blessed are those who are called to the Marriage Feast of the Lamb"* (Rev 19:9).

References

Catechism of the Catholic Church:
ccc. 1322-1419 (*Compendium* questions 271-294)

Further reading:
ARINZE, F., *The Holy Eucharist*, Emmaus Road; HARDON, J., *With Us Today*, Veritas Press; VONIER, A., *A Key to the Doctrine of the Eucharist*, Ignatius Press

Confession and Anointing

If you forgive the sins of any, they are forgiven.

John 20:23

*e*VANGELIUM

What is Confession?

Confession (or *Penance* or *Reconciliation*) is the sacrament by which we, repenting and confessing our sins, are absolved of sin through the ministry of a priest.

Why is Confession important?

Confession is important because it is the normal way we can be forgiven serious sin after Baptism.

Regular Confession is important because it helps us to deal with our sins quickly and to develop a mature conscience. It also gives grace to resist temptation. The act of confessing itself bestows healing and a sense of release from the burden of sin.

How did Christ establish Confession?

Scripture states that only God can forgive sins (Mk 2:7). However, Jesus Christ gave his power to forgive sins to his apostles. The format of the sacrament has varied over time; however, the requirement for priestly absolution and (except when the penitent is incapable) verbal confession has remained constant. By these means, the mercy that Christ brought is perpetuated until the end of time.

He breathed on them, and said to them, "Receive the Holy Spirit. If you forgive the sins of any, they are forgiven; if you retain the sins of any, they are retained."   Jn 20:22-23

Confession and Reconciliation

Confession is also called Reconciliation. Sin damages our relationship with God and with the Church. It is this sacrament that reconciles us once again.

God's willingness to forgive us even after Baptism is expressed powerfully in the parable of the prodigal son welcomed home by his father, *"My son was dead, and is alive again; he was lost, and is found"* (Lk 15:24).

The Return of the Prodigal Son by Rembrandt

Repairing the damage of sin

The damage caused by sin needs to be repaired even after the guilt of the sin itself has been forgiven by absolution. For this reason the priest will give a penance in the Confession. This is generally a prayer, a work of mercy, a sacrifice or an act of self-denial. By the mercy of God, these acts remove the punishment we deserve due to the effects of our sins. Indulgences offered by the Church are another means of remitting this punishment.

THE ACTIONS OF THE PENITENT	THE ESSENTIAL WORDS OF THE PRIEST
Contrition: being sorry for my sins and having a firm intention to avoid them in future.	After hearing my confession of sins, giving me a penance for reparation and hearing my act of contrition, the priest gives me absolution:
Verbal confession of sins: the telling of the kinds of sins I have committed and the number of times I have committed them. I must include all my mortal sins.	*God, the Father of mercies, through the death and resurrection of His Son has reconciled the world to himself and sent the Holy Spirit among us for the forgiveness of sins; through the ministry of the Church may God grant you pardon and peace,*
Will to make reparation: the intention to repair the damage caused by my sins, and to fulfil the penance set by the priest.	*and I absolve you from your sins in the name of the Father, and of the Son, and of the Holy Spirit. Amen*

The Lord Jesus Christ, physician of our souls and bodies ... has willed that His Church continue, in the power of the Holy Spirit, His work of healing and salvation, even among her own members. This is the purpose of the two sacraments of healing: the sacrament of Penance and the sacrament of Anointing of the Sick.

Catechism of the Catholic Church n. 1421

What is the Sacrament of Anointing of the Sick?

The Anointing of the Sick is that sacrament by which sick persons, through anointing with oil and the prayer of the priest, receive grace for the salvation of their souls and possible bodily healing.

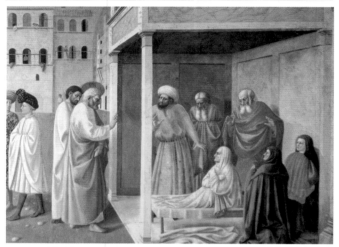

The Healing of the Cripple and Raising of Tabatha by Masolino da Panicale

Why is Anointing of the Sick important?

Anointing is important because it strengthens our souls and bodies at the approach of death, either to heal us or to help us to die in a state of grace.

This is a crucial help because the condition of our souls at death completes our earthly pilgrimage and fixes our state for eternity.

How did Christ establish Anointing?

Scripture describes Jesus as the physician of our souls and bodies and during his earthly ministry he healed the sick both spiritually and physically. He promised that his disciples would also lay hands on the sick, who would recover (Mk 16:17-18).

The Letter of James bears witness to the fact that the first priests of the Church anointed the sick:

Is any man sick among you? Let him bring in the priests of the church and let them pray over him, anointing him with oil in the name of the Lord. And the prayer of faith shall save the sick man. And the Lord shall raise him up: and if he be in sins, they shall be forgiven him. Jas 5:14-15 DRA

What are the effects of Anointing?

THE EFFECTS OF ANOINTING	
The strengthening of the sick person	Anointing strengthens the soul of the sick person by awakening confidence in God's mercy. It also gives the strength to bear suffering and resist temptation. Someone who offers their suffering to God in union with Christ can aid their own salvation and assist that of others, *"in my flesh I complete what is lacking in Christ's afflictions for the sake of his body, that is, the church"* (Col 1:24). When the Eucharist accompanies Anointing it is called *viaticum*, 'food for the journey'.
The remission of sins	Anointing remits sins. It takes away venial sins and, when the person is incapable of confessing, it can take away mortal sins as well. The sacrament of Confession often accompanies Anointing.
The healing of the body	God intends Anointing to help us achieve salvation. The sacrament does, therefore, heal our bodies when this is to our spiritual advantage. It is not God's will, however, that we ultimately avoid natural death, which is now our means of entry to eternal life.

How is Anointing given?

The proper time to receive Anointing is when a person is seriously ill and in danger of death from sickness or old age. Anointing should not be delayed until the point of death, however, and if the person subsequently recovers and relapses later, he or she can receive the sacrament again.

The priest lays his hands on the sick person and then anoints him or her with the blessed oil. First he anoints the forehead while speaking the words, *"Through this holy anointing may the Lord in his love and mercy help you with the grace of the Holy Spirit."* Then he anoints the hands with the words, *"May the Lord who frees you from sin save you and raise you up."*

References

<u>Catechism of the Catholic Church</u>:
ccc. 1420-1532 (*Compendium* questions 295-320)

<u>Further reading</u>:
RANDOLPH, F., *Pardon and Peace*, Ignatius; HAHN S., *Lord Have Mercy: The Healing Power of Confession*, DLT; BERTRAM, J., *Anointing*, CTS; DAVANZO, G., *Giving Meaning to suffering*, CTS

Marriage and Holy Orders

Blessed are those who are invited to the Wedding Feast of the Lamb.
Revelation 19:9 NJB

*e*VANGELIUM

The Sacrament of Marriage

Marriage is that sacrament by which a baptised man and woman are bound together by vows to an exclusive lifelong commitment to one another and to accepting and raising children. In this sacrament God gives grace for the fulfilment of these duties.

What are the roots of Marriage?

God created human beings as male and female. This complementarity is the natural basis of Marriage, which throughout history has provided a stable, loving environment for the procreation and raising of children. Marriage is naturally monogamous and indissoluble but, due to the Fall, polygamy and divorce have often been tolerated. Jesus says this was not God's intention in creation:

From the beginning of creation, 'God made them male and female.' For this reason a man shall leave his father and mother and be joined to his wife, and the two shall become one flesh. So they are no longer two but one flesh. What therefore God has joined together, let not man put asunder."

Mk 10:2-9

Christ and the sacrament of Marriage

The Catechism affirms that Marriage was "*raised by Christ the Lord to the dignity of a Sacrament*" (ccc. 1601).

When a man and woman are baptised, they become members of the Church which is the 'Bride of Christ'. This relationship of Christ with his Church is then made present in their sacramental Marriage, marking it with a specifically Christian character. St Paul confirms this by referring to Marriage as a *mystērion*, which can be translated as 'sacrament'.

For this reason a man shall leave his father and mother and be joined to his wife, and the two shall become one flesh. This mystery (mystērion) is a profound one, and I am saying that it refers to Christ and the church.

Eph 5:31-32

The Marriage at Cana by Giotto di Bondone

This link with Christ and the Church implies:

- **Joy** in loving union, and a foretaste of the 'Wedding Feast of the Lamb' (Rev. 19:7).

- **Sacrifice**, in that the spouses follow Christ in giving their lives for each other unto death.

- **Fruitfulness**, in both the growth in holiness of the spouses and acceptance of children.

What is necessary for the sacrament?

The spouses confer the sacrament on one another. They must vow freely, have no impediments (such as previous valid marriages), be committed to one another for life and be open to children from God. Following the established rite, each must say, "*I take you ...*" in the presence of a minister and witnesses.

As Marriage is indissoluble until death, divorce is impossible. An *annulment* is the recognition by the Church that there was never a valid Marriage.

All valid Marriages between Christians are sacramental. When both spouses practice the same Catholic faith, however, they share a common, supernatural vision for their relationship and receive many blessings.

Two other sacraments, Holy Orders and Matrimony, are directed towards the salvation of others; if they contribute as well to personal salvation, it is through service to others that they do so. They confer a particular mission in the Church and serve to build up the People of God.

Catechism of the Catholic Church n. 1534

The Sacrament of Holy Orders

Holy Orders is the sacrament in which a baptised man receives the authority and ability to share in the particular mission that Christ entrusted to his apostles. There are three orders of this sacrament: episcopate, presbyterate and diaconate.

The sacrament is conferred through the laying on of hands and the consecratory prayer of the bishop according to the rite of the Church.

The Ordination of Saint Lawrence by Fra Angelico

Where do Holy Orders come from?

Jesus called disciples to follow him in a variety of ways, shown forth today by the many forms of lay, consecrated and ordained ministry and service. From among his disciples, Jesus set aside twelve men, the 'apostles', specially ordaining them to:

- **Govern** with his authority, "*Whatever you bind on earth will be bound in heaven*" (Mt 18:18).

- **Teach** in his name, "*Make disciples … teaching them to observe all that I have commanded you*" (Mt 28:19-20).

- **Sanctify** with the power of his sacraments, "*Do this in memory of me*" (Lk 22:19).

How are Holy Orders passed on?

The apostles conferred Holy Orders on their successors, the bishops; they in turn conferred the sacrament to ordain priests and deacons. Today in the person of Christ those in Holy Orders:

- **Govern** – by uniting, protecting and leading the faithful to their heavenly homeland.

- **Teach** – by preaching and explaining Scripture and Tradition with authority.

- **Sanctify** – by conferring the sacraments and interceding with God for his people.

THE THREE SACRAMENTAL ORDERS

Bishops are the successors of the apostles. They usually govern dioceses, can confer Holy Orders on others, and normally administer Confirmation. Together with the Pope they exercise an infallible teaching authority for the whole Church.

Priests are co-workers of the bishops, particularly as governors and teachers of parishes (where they are properly called 'Father'). They sanctify the faithful through the celebration of the Eucharist, the forgiveness of sins in Confession, Baptism and the Anointing of the Sick. They also preside at Marriages.

Deacons assist the work of the bishop and his priests, especially by assisting at the altar, proclaiming the gospel and works of charity. While a promise of lifelong celibacy is the normal condition for reception of Holy Orders, a permanent deacon may be married.

The call to Holy Orders

Jesus has said explicitly that the call to Holy Orders is his initiative rather than ours, "*You did not choose me, but I chose you*" (Jn 15:16). The call is discerned and freely accepted by the man who receives it. The Church tests this call and prepares the candidate for Holy Orders by means of spiritual, human, academic and pastoral formation, usually in a seminary.

For every high priest taken from among men is ordained for men in the things that appertain to God, that he may offer up gifts and sacrifices for sins. Heb 5:1

References
<u>Catechism of the Catholic Church</u>:
ccc. 1533-1666 (*Compendium* questions 321-350)

<u>Further reading</u>:
Familiaris Consortio, Catholic Truth Society; WOJTYLA, K., *Love and Responsibility*, Ignatius Press; MARKS, F. W., *Catholic Handbook for Engaged and Newly Married Couples*, Emmaus Road; SHEEN, F. J., *The Priest is Not His Own*, Ignatius Press; DOLAN, T. M., *Priests for the Third Millennium*, Our Sunday Visitor

Moral Action

I have set before you life and death, blessing and curse; therefore choose life.
Deuteronomy 30:19

What is a Moral Action?

A moral action is any action that proceeds from our deliberate will. We have responsibility for such actions, all of which are either good or evil.

One of our unique abilities as human beings is to direct our own lives. We are free to choose our actions; we are not simply determined by instinct.

This freedom enables us to be creative and to choose from among many possible good actions.

You may freely eat of every tree of the garden. Gen 2:16

Unfortunately, this freedom also enables us to choose things that are evil, that is, contrary to what is good for us and to what God commands.

But of the tree of the knowledge of good and evil you shall not eat, for in the day that you eat of it you shall die. Gen 2:17

God greatly desires us to choose only what is good for us, because he has created us out of love to be his adopted children, free, holy and happy with him forever. God does not, however, force us to do good. As long as we are alive here, we remain free to choose between good and evil. The effects of both kinds of choice are evident in human society.

What is sin?

A sin is a deliberate evil action: a thought, word, deed or omission contrary to God's will.

All sins are acts contrary to the will of God. They either pervert some aspect of our human nature that he has created (such as greedy, slothful or lustful acts) or contravene some explicit command that he has given us (such as the prohibition against eating the fruit of the tree of knowledge (Gen 2:17)).

The root of all sin is *pride*, the attempt to make oneself into one's own 'god' independent of the order of nature and the obedience we owe to God.

The Fall and Expulsion from the Garden of Eden by Michaelangelo

Mortal and venial sin

Although all sin is evil, not all sin is equally evil. A sin is **mortal** if all the following conditions are present.

Grave matter	What we do, i.e. our chosen course of action, is gravely wrong.
Knowledge	We know full well, or should know, that this action is seriously evil.
Full consent	We freely consent to this action and could clearly have done otherwise.

Such sin is 'mortal' because it kills the divine life of the soul and deprives the sinner of heaven. The normal remedy for this sin is the sacrament of Confession.

All other sins are **venial**. They do not kill the divine life of the soul but they do damage and weaken us. Venial sins may be forgiven through Confession, in the Mass or through personal prayers of repentance.

How can we do what is good?

One of the consequences of Original Sin is that it is not easy for us to do what is good. We tend to desire sinful things, a condition called *disordered concupiscence*.

A good *conscience*, formed through study of the moral law and good example, helps us to judge what is right. Establishing good habits in a well-ordered life and avoiding temptations also help us. However, it is only with God's grace, through the sacraments and prayer, that we can achieve final victory over sin.

Finding himself in the midst of the battlefield man has to struggle to do what is right, and it is a great cost to himself, and aided by God's grace, that he succeeds in achieving his own integrity.

Gaudium et Spes n. 37 § 2; Catechism of the Catholic Church n. 409

Moral Battle and Victory

What is the great battle?

The great battle is the struggle between good and evil which takes place daily in our lives.

Our opponents are the world, the flesh and the devil. These conspire to intimidate us and tempt us away from following Jesus Christ. Our ultimate happiness depends on achieving victory over them.

The world, the flesh and the devil

There are two senses in which Christians understand 'the world'. In the first sense the world is good since it is created by God. Unfortunately, however, there are now evil influences in the world opposed to God's will and our good actions. These influences are also collectively referred to as 'the world'.

The world is our enemy in this second sense, because it encourages evil and discourages good.

Temptations	Examples
Ideas and slogans	*"You only live once!"*
Empty pleasures	Rich and selfish living
Evil examples	Immoral public figures
Intimidations	
Mental persecutions	Peer pressure and ridicule
Physical persecutions	Unjust laws, physical harm

The flesh is an enemy because of evil concupiscence. Pleasures are good things created by God. However, a disordered and unrestrained pursuit of pleasure in our fallen condition risks dominating our lives and enslaving us to sin. In addition, the fear of pain may prevent us from doing the good that we should do.

Temptations	Examples
Disordered desires for certain things	Eating disorders, sex or drug addictions
Intimidations	
Disordered fears of certain things	The fear of effort, hostile reactions or sacrifice

The devil and his fallen angels are our spiritual enemies because of their hatred of God and their desire to deprive us of eternal happiness.

These creatures also have intellects that they use in a perverted way against us. As well as acting directly, they also use the world and the flesh against us. For this reason, the attacks against Christians often seem to be organised in a strategic way.

Temptations	Examples
Empty promises	*"If you will, then, worship me, it shall all be yours"* (Lk 4:7).
Lies	*"You will not die"* (Gen 3:4).
Intimidations	
Threats	State terror (1 Macc 1)
Confusion	Evil prophets (Mt 13:22)

The victory of Christ

All Christians face temptations and intimidations in following Jesus Christ. However, Christ himself has conquered the world, the flesh and the devil.

The Temptation of Christ by Duccio di Buoninsegna

If we call on God's help and use the aids he has given us in Scripture and the Church, we shall have all we need to fight and win the great battle.

"In the world you face persecution. But take courage; I have conquered the world"
Jn 16:33

References

Catechism of the Catholic Church:
ccc. 407-409; 1264; 1730-1748; 1749-1761; 1776-1802; 1846-1876 (*Compendium* questions 363-376; 391-400)

Further reading:
LONGENECKER, D. *The Great Battle*, CTS; MAY, W., *An Introduction to Moral Theology*, Our Sunday Visitor; GROESCHEL, B., *Arise from Darkness*, Ignatius Press

The Natural Law and the Ten Commandments

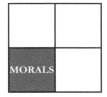

MORALS

If you would enter life, keep the commandments. Matthew 19:17

The Natural Law

> The natural law, known by reason, is the universal moral law of human nature for living well.

The natural law is 'natural' because it is founded on what is good for human nature and because we can know it by our natural faculty of reason.

The natural law is valid for all people in all societies. Its principles can be understood by reason, even without faith. For example, dishonouring parents, murder, theft, adultery and lying are recognised by practically all human societies as being contrary to what is good for human life.

Christians have a duty to uphold the precepts of the natural law, both because these are rational and good in themselves and because they are part of God's will for us, 'written' into our shared human nature.

> *When Gentiles who have not the law do by nature what the law requires, they are a law to themselves, even though they do not have the law. They show that what the law requires is written on their hearts.*
> Rom 2:14-15

Natural and civil law

Civil laws apply the principles of natural law to determine what is good for particular societies.

For example, the natural law forbids murder. Many more detailed civil laws are required, however, to extend this principle to defining, for instance, good medical practice and legitimate action in war.

Christians have a duty to promote good legislation and to obey the civil laws of the societies they live in.

> *"Everyone is to obey the governing authorities."* Rom 13:1 NJB

Nevertheless, particular civil laws can sometimes violate natural law, examples being the racial laws of Nazi Germany or laws permitting the killing of the unborn. Legitimate civil laws can never oblige anyone to commit sin (cf. ccc. 1903).

The Ten Commandments

The Ten Commandments contain God's specific codification of the main principles of the natural law.

God revealed these commandments (Ex 20:2-17; Deut 5:6-21) of the natural law because Original Sin made it hard for human beings to discern good from evil. The commandments also make clear rules for living out the general principles of natural law, such as the need to set aside a specific time for God.

Moses by Guido Reni

Jesus Christ said that he had not come to abolish the law, but to fulfil it (Mt 5:17). In particular, he confirmed the necessity of the Ten Commandments.

> *Someone came to him and said, "Teacher, what good deed must I do to have eternal life?" And he said to him ... "If you wish to enter into life, keep the commandments."*
> Mt 19:16-17

The natural law and the law of grace

In addition to the Ten Commandments, Christians also follow the new 'law of grace', prefigured by certain additional Old Testament precepts God gave to Israel. By the 'law of grace' God directs us to the supernatural happiness of the kingdom of heaven.

The essence of the law of grace is to follow Jesus Christ in his Church, putting our possessions and lives at the service of God and others in charity.

> *"If you wish to be perfect, go, sell your possessions, and give the money to the poor, and you will have treasure in heaven; then come, follow me."*
> Mt 19:21 NRSV

A full explanation of the Commandments of the Decalogue became necessary in the state of sin because the light of reason was obscured and the will had gone astray.
Catechism of the Catholic Church n. 2071

The Ten Commandments (Decalogue)

The Ten Commandments are the ten universal laws given directly by God to Moses on Mount Sinai.

	COMMANDMENT	EXPLANATION	BIBLICAL EXAMPLES	MODERN EXAMPLES
1	**I am the Lord your God; you shall not have strange gods before me.**	God, as our creator, wants us to love him above all else.	The people of Israel worshipped the golden calf (Ex 32:1-20).	Using magic, occult or superstitious practices (e.g. horoscopes); syncretism; giving priority to anything other than God.
2	**You shall not take the name of the Lord your God in vain.**	God's name and all things dedicated to him should not be misused or treated lightly.	The money changers in the temple (Mk 11:15-17)	Misusing holy names as swear words; breaking oaths; disrespect for holy places, objects or persons.
3	**Remember to keep holy the Lord's day.**	God wants us to dedicate specific time to him since worship is of the greatest importance.	The failure to keep the Sabbath in the time of the prophets (Jer 17:19-27).	Missing Mass on Sunday or a holy day; doing unnecessary business or work on this day.
4	**Honour your father and your mother.**	The family is the basis of society. Respect is due to parents and other lawful authorities.	The prodigal son in the parable told by Jesus (Lk 15:11-32).	Refusing to love our parents and obey lawful authority; neglecting elderly parents.
5	**You shall not kill.**	To destroy or harm human life, made in God's image, is a rejection of God's gift, the person and society.	Cain killed his brother Abel (Gen 4:1-12).	Murder; abortion; IVF; euthanasia; unjust war; failure to provide for those in severe poverty.
6	**You shall not commit adultery.**	Marriage is a sacred bond which cannot be broken. It is the only context for sexual acts.	Herod lived unlawfully with Herodias, his brother's wife (Mk 6:17-18).	Adultery; masturbation; homosexual acts; artificial contraception; living together before Marriage.
7	**You shall not steal.**	Personal property is needed for human well-being. Stealing is an attack on personal and civic life.	Pharaoh stole from the Israelites by using them as slave labour (Ex 1:8-14).	Unlawfully taking things; not paying taxes and debts; not paying just wages.
8	**You shall not bear false witness against your neighbour.**	To attack a person's reputation is an attack on human dignity and leads to injustice.	The false witnesses at Jesus' trial (Mk 14:55-59).	Lying about someone in a law court; gossip; calumny or detraction of another's good name.
9	**You shall not covet your neighbour's wife.**	To desire evil is itself evil, and impure thoughts corrupt our minds and can lead to immoral actions.	King David unlawfully desired Bathsheba, the wife of one of his soldiers. (2 Sam 11:2-4).	Thinking of people as sexual objects; use of pornographic literature or images; impure fantasies.
10	**You shall not covet your neighbour's goods.**	God wants us to make full use of the gifts he has given us, not to desire the gifts of others instead.	The brothers of Joseph were jealous of his status and his robe (Gen 37:3-11).	Jealousy of another's talents and possessions. Being ungrateful to God for his gifts to us.

References

Catechism of the Catholic Church:
ccc. 1949-1964; 2052-2557 (*Compendium* questions 415-421; 434-533)

Further reading:
POPE JOHN PAUL II, *Veritatis Splendor*, Catholic Truth Society; PELL, G. CARDINAL, *Issues of Faith and Morals*, Ignatius Press

Grace and the Beatitudes

He has given us his very great and precious promises, so that through them you may participate in the divine nature! 2 Peter 1:4

What is Grace?

Grace refers to those gifts that bring about a supernatural friendship of a person with God. *Supernatural* means an elevation of human nature beyond what it is naturally capable of attaining.

All grace comes to us from God by means of Jesus Christ and his Church. The life of grace begins in Baptism, which is a supernatural birth:

"Very truly, I tell you, no one can see the kingdom of God without being born from above." Jn 3:3 NRSV

By means of this extraordinary gift, God allows us to share his own divine life, as his adopted children, and makes us heirs to the kingdom of heaven.

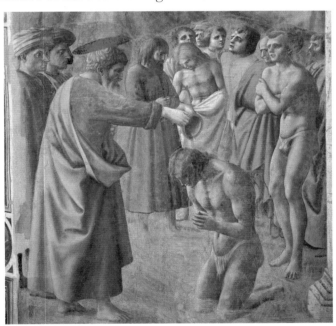

The Baptism of the Neophytes by Masaccio

In referring to this supernatural life, St Peter says we become *partakers of the divine nature* (2 Pet 1:4). St Paul calls us *co-heirs of Christ* (Rom 8:17) and *temples of the Holy Spirit* (1 Cor 3:16). The Church Fathers refer to this gift as *divinisation*, and our elevation to this state is the principal aspect of our *justification* in Christ.

The life of grace

Just as natural human life develops towards maturity, so too does the life of grace. Far from being a parallel and disconnected life, however, grace builds on our human nature and brings it to perfection in heaven.

LIFE OF NATURE	LIFE OF GRACE
Natural birth	Baptism
Philosophical virtues (for example, prudence)	Theological virtues (faith, hope, charity)
Food and drink	The Eucharist
Human society	The Church
Growth to adulthood	Growth in holiness
Human happiness	The vision of God

The theological virtues *"dispose Christians to live in a relationship with the Holy Trinity. They have God for their origin, their motive and their object – God known by Faith, God Hoped in and God Loved for His own sake."* (ccc. 1840)

There are two main kinds of grace. *Sanctifying* grace makes us children of God. *Actual* grace refers to the particular prompts and assistance that God gives us to help us act in ways leading to holiness.

Mortal sin causes the loss of sanctifying grace, which can, however, be restored by means of Confession.

Mistakes regarding grace

☒ **Pelagianism**	That we can save ourselves. 'Grace' is therefore only the forgiveness of sins and the example of Christ.
☒ **Determinism**	That 'grace' determines absolutely the eternal outcome of our lives. Free will has no significant role.
☒ **Modernism**	That 'grace' is the same as nature. By nature we are one with God, or *part* of God or gradually *making* God.

What no eye has seen, nor ear heard, nor the heart of man conceived, what God has prepared for those who love him.

1 Corinthians 2:9

What are the Beatitudes?

The Beatitudes are eight states of blessedness proclaimed by Christ in the Sermon on the Mount (Mt 5:3-11). These states manifest the life of heaven on earth, bringing a foretaste and promise of joy even amid earthly suffering.

Blessed are the poor in spirit, for theirs is the kingdom of heaven.	Poverty of spirit enables us not only to use the goods of this world (such as riches and honours) in moderation, but to be willing to surrender all of them joyfully for the sake of the kingdom of heaven.
	Jesus said to him, "If you would be perfect, go, sell what you possess and give to the poor, and you will have treasure in heaven; and come, follow me." Mt 19:21
Blessed are those who mourn, for they shall be comforted.	Mourning might not seem like a state of blessedness because earthly joys are not bad in themselves, although they can still come to dominate our lives. However, by grace we set our hearts on heaven and are dissatisfied with anything less.
	"Truly, truly, I say to you, you will weep and lament, but the world will rejoice; you will be sorrowful, but your sorrow will turn into joy." Jn 16:20
Blessed are the meek, for they shall inherit the earth.	Meekness refuses even a proportionate and just response to evil. Jesus showed us the meaning of meekness when he submitted to being scourged, mocked and crucified without striking back.
	"To him who strikes you on the cheek, offer the other also; and from him who takes away your coat do not withhold even your shirt." Lk 6:29
Blessed are those who hunger and thirst for righteousness, for they shall be satisfied.	Hunger and thirst for righteousness goes beyond doing our duties to our neighbour. It is an *eager desire*, like a bodily appetite when we hunger and thirst, to do works of mercy, so that those around us and ourselves grow in holiness.
	"Seek first his kingdom and his righteousness, and all these things shall be yours as well." Mt 6:31-33
Blessed are the merciful, for they shall obtain mercy.	Mercy exceeds natural benevolence and natural pardon for wrongdoing. It is a lavish bestowing of our time and goods on those who cannot repay us. It is also the gift of forgiving even outrageous wrongs against us.
	"When you give a feast, invite the poor, the maimed, the lame, the blind, and you will be blessed, because they cannot repay you" (Lk 14:13-14). *"Love your enemies."* Mt 5:43-44
Blessed are the pure in heart, for they shall see God.	Purity of heart is far more than preserving oneself from the stain of sin. It is the gift of a God-like heart, to love God for his own sake with a single minded clarity and passion, and to love others as God loves them.
	"A new commandment I give to you, that you love one another; even as I have loved you, that you also love one another." Jn 13:34-35
Blessed are the peacemakers, for they shall be called sons of God.	Peacemaking goes beyond mere tranquil good order in earthly relationships. It is the gift of establishing unity with others in a friendship founded on the desire for their supernatural good, that is, to reach our final home with God in heaven.
	"Peace I leave with you; my peace I give to you; not as the world gives do I give to you. Let not your hearts be troubled, neither let them be afraid." Jn 14:27
Blessed are those who are persecuted for righteousness' sake ... be glad, for your reward is great in heaven.	Persecution refers specifically to the trials that Christians face for preaching and living the Gospel. It blesses us in that it conforms us to Christ crucified, and holds the promise of great reward in heaven.
	"I have said this to you, so that in me you may have peace. In the world you face persecution. But take courage; I have conquered the world!" Jn 16:33

References

Catechism of the Catholic Church:
CCC. 1716-1729; 1812-1835; 1987-2029 (*Compendium* questions 358-362; 384-390; 422-428)

Further reading:
SHEEN, F. J., *The Cross and the Beatitudes*, Ligouri Publications; JOURNET, C., *The Meaning of Grace*, Scepter Publishers; SCHEEBEN, M., *The Glories of Divine Grace*, TAN

Virtues and Vices

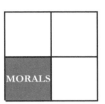

It is she (Wisdom) who teaches temperance and prudence, justice and fortitude.

Wisdom 8:7

What are Virtues?

> Virtues are good habits, that is, they give us a disposition to perform good actions.

Our actions as human beings are not simply a sequence of disconnected choices. We develop or acquire interior dispositions or habits, which *incline* us to perform particular kinds of actions. When these habits are good we call them virtues.

What are the principal virtues?

There are four principal natural human virtues which every good person needs. These are the **cardinal virtues** of *prudence* (also called *practical wisdom*), *fortitude, temperance* and *justice*. All moral virtues are linked to the cardinal virtues, which are connected together, in the Christian life of grace, by charity.

In addition to the cardinal virtues, there are three virtues which are unique to the Christian life of grace after Baptism. These are the 'supernatural' (or 'theological') virtues of *faith, hope* and *charity (love)*.

Charity is lost if grace is lost through mortal sin; it is restored by means of Confession. Charity is the supernatural virtue of heaven, *"So faith, hope, love abide, these three; but the greatest of these is love"* (1 Cor 13:13).

How do we achieve the virtues?

To some extent, a person can acquire the natural virtues through the personal discipline of repeated good actions and a well-ordered life.

In our fallen condition, however, it is not even possible to achieve complete human perfection by our own efforts. It is only the perfection given by grace, by means of the sacraments and prayer, which also enables us to achieve the cardinal virtues.

Prudence

The virtue of deliberating well about what actions we should do.

Prudence or practical wisdom directs us about what we should do in particular, practical situations.

Since moral laws do not determine every possible action we might take, we also need prudence to direct our choice of actions well.

Fortitude

The virtue of constancy in holding fast to good actions even when they are difficult.

Fortitude strengthens us against withdrawing from the good we should do in particular situations.

Since it is not enough just to know what is right; we also need fortitude to carry out our good actions.

Justice

The virtue of rendering to each and to all what belongs to them.

Justice enables us to act justly in accordance with what practical reason directs us to do.

Since we are social by nature, we should seek the perfection of the societies in which we live. For this we need the virtue of justice.

Temperance

The virtue of curbing the passions that incite us to evil actions.

Temperance prevents us from yielding to our disordered desires and therefore pursuing what is evil.

Since our disordered desires lead to temptations, we need temperance to avoid evil in these situations.

The Seven Virtues (details: prudence, justice, temperance, fortitude) by Giotto di Bondone

Above all these put on love which binds everything together in perfect harmony.

Colossians 3:14

What are Vices?

Vices are evil habits; that is, they give us a disposition to perform evil actions.

We sometimes develop vices which incline us to perform evil actions. These normally involve excess or deficiency in pursuing what is good.

The seven deadly vices

The most well-known and traditional list of vices is called the **seven deadly sins** or **vices**.

These vices are called deadly because of their poisonous effects on the human soul, the difficulty that is often experienced in eradicating them, and the ease with which they lead to mortal sin. They are also called *capital sins*, because they give rise to many other kinds of sins by those who commit them.

The Seven Deadly Sins by Hieronymous Bosch

Each of these vices has, as a remedy, a contrary virtue linked to the cardinal virtues. The vices may promise an easier life but they ensnare and enslave us. The virtues may seem difficult, but they lead to our true freedom and happiness as human beings.

Make every effort to supplement your faith with virtue.

2 Pet 1:5

The vices and their remedies

PRIDE	HUMILITY
Ascribing an excellence to oneself that one does not possess, or believing one is the cause of one's own excellence, or a desire to be singularly and conspicuously great, despising everyone else.	*A recognition that we are created by God and in need of his love and help; it helps us to form a true opinion of ourselves, to disregard shallow popularity and to free us from self-obsession.*
ENVY	FRATERNAL CHARITY
A grieving or sorrow for the goods and blessings given to others, insofar as their gifts differ from or surpass our own.	*A gratitude for the gifts and talents of others and a desire that each and every person reaches their full potential.*
ANGER	MEEKNESS
A violent passion to inflict revenge on others, to the point of clouding one's reason and usurping God's judgment.	*A self-control inspired by God's clemency, which allows us to master our emotions when attacked or wronged.*
SLOTH	DILIGENCE
A laziness, spiritual torpor or oppressive sorrow that prevents us from doing what we can achieve and should do.	*An eagerness to do what is needed inspired by the zeal of divine love, making even difficult tasks achievable.*
AVARICE	LIBERALITY
A disordered desire for riches and possessions, to the point of acting contrary to the love of God and neighbour.	*A generosity towards others in sharing God's gifts; it brings personal contentment with whatever we possess.*
GLUTTONY	TEMPERANCE
A disordered desire to consume food and drink too sumptuously, too much, too hastily, greedily or daintily.	*A good order in desiring the pleasures of taste and touch, inspired by respect for oneself as a temple of the Holy Spirit.*
LUST	CHASTITY
A disordered craving for sexual pleasure leading to abuses of the body and mind, addictions and destructive effects on families and society.	*A proper use of our sexuality. It guards our hearts and minds from evil influences, gives us freedom and allows us to love God and others purely.*

References

Catechism of the Catholic Church:
ccc. 1803-1829; 1833-1844 (*Compendium* questions 377-383)

Further reading:
KREEFT, P., *Back to Virtue*, Ignatius Press, 1992; PIEPER, JOSEPH, *The Four Cardinal Virtues*, Notre Dame, 1966; *A Brief Reader on the Virtues of the Human Heart*, Ignatius, 1991; CASSIAN, ST JOHN, *On the Training of a Monk and the Eight Deadly Sins*, The Saint Austin Press, 1999

Christian Life in the World

Follow me!
Matthew 4:19

MORALS

The Personal Christian Life

The personal Christian life is the conforming of one's life to the pattern of Jesus Christ.

Personal prayer life

Fidelity to a pattern of daily prayer is essential to the effective living of the Christian life. While the prayer of each Christian will reflect his or her particular circumstances and needs, the Church and her saints give us certain common principles of daily prayer:

- Pray each day, preferably at set times and especially at the beginning and end of the day.

- Learn some of the most important prayers, so that they can be recalled easily at any time.

- Practise clearing the mind of distractions and turning to God even in daily work.

It is better to begin by devoting short daily periods to prayer than to pray for long periods but to do so only occasionally.

Personal knowledge

Knowledge is essential to living the Christian life, because we cannot love what we do not know. It is therefore helpful to our development to:

- Set aside time for reading Scripture and other books about the faith.

- Share and discuss the faith with others, particularly priests and teachers.

- Attend a catechetical course and make use of other Catholic educational resources.

Christ Carrying His Cross by Stanley Spencer

Personal sacramental life

Since the sacraments begin and sustain the Christian life it is beneficial to go to Mass and Confession more often than is obligatory. Daily Mass and monthly Confession are recommended practices.

Personal moral life

Personal morality is essential to living in an authentic Christian way and remaining in God's grace. God calls us to follow his will even in our smallest actions and to offer daily sacrifices for ourselves and others. The lives of the saints teach us to:

- Ask God for the grace each day to grow in virtue and avoid vice.

- Make an examination of conscience and moral resolutions at the end of each day.

- Make specific acts of charity and sacrifice, such as fasting.

SIX PRECEPTS OF THE CHURCH: THE OBLIGATORY MINIMUM FOR THE PERSONAL CHRISTIAN LIFE	
1. You shall attend Mass on Sundays and holy days of obligation.	4. You shall keep holy the holy days of obligation.
2. You shall receive the sacrament of Confession (Reconciliation) at least once a year.	5. You shall fast and observe abstinence on the prescribed days.
3. You shall receive Holy Communion at least once during the Easter season.	6. You shall provide for the material needs of the Church according to your ability.

All Christians … are called to the fullness of Christian life and to the perfection of charity.

Lumen Gentium 40.2

The Public Christian Life

The public Christian life is the conforming of one's own family and society to the pattern of Jesus Christ.

Christian society

We are called to pray and work for a Christian society that respects natural law, upholds the dignity of all people, is conducive to evangelisation and encourages everyone to follow their God-given vocations.

Vocation

Every human being is called to a particular kind of service. Marriage is the vocation of most people, although some are called to remain single. God also specifically calls some people to consecrate themselves in religious life or the priesthood.

To discern and follow our vocation we need to:

- Pray to discover God's will for us.

- Examine our talents and the contemporary needs of the Church and the world.

- Pray for the strength to pursue our vocation when it has become clear to us.

Evangelisation

We have a responsibility to proclaim the Gospel to others, a proclamation which is called evangelisation. We evangelise in a variety of ways, such as:

- Praying for the conversion and spiritual growth of others.

- Teaching the faith to our families and friends, where most evangelisation takes place.

- Being ready to introduce others to the faith in a variety of ways, such as conversations, books and above all by good example.

Acts of charity

We are commanded by Christ to practice charity in Christian living. In particular, the practice of the works of mercy promotes Christian justice and true peace in society. There are seven principal corporal and seven principal spiritual works of mercy.

CORPORAL WORKS OF MERCY	SPIRITUAL WORKS OF MERCY
Feed the hungry	Convert the sinner
Give drink to the thirsty	Instruct the ignorant
Clothe the naked	Counsel the doubtful
Harbour the homeless	Comfort the sorrowful
Visit the sick	Bear wrongs patiently
Visit the imprisoned	Forgive injustice
Bury the dead	Pray for the living and dead

Challenging the 'culture of death'

The attitudes and laws of many states have changed in ways that are contrary to respect for human life.

☒ **Abortion**	Abortion is the intentional killing of a child between conception and birth. It attacks the sanctity of a life made in the image of God.
☒ **Euthanasia and suicide**	Euthanasia is killing as a false act of mercy, a practice that corrodes respect for the old and infirm and can soon become involuntary. Suicide is the intentional killing of oneself. They hinder God's completion of a life.
☒ **Cloning and IVF**	Human cloning is the artificial duplication of human beings. In vitro fertilisation (IVF) is artificial non-sexual procreation. They attack the dignity of the child, the sanctity of natural procreation and lead in practice to the mass destruction of embryos.
☒ **Divorce, re-marriage and cohabitation**	Divorce, re-marriage and cohabitation all destabilise and devalue the dignity of Marriage and the family as the natural foundations of society.
☒ **Artificial contraception; homosexual activity**	Artificial contraception and homosexual activity separate the gift of human sexuality from procreation or from married love altogether, contributing to a sexually irresponsible and sterile culture.

It is a work of mercy to avoid these practices ourselves and to help others avoid them by word and example.

References

Catechism of the Catholic Church:
ccc. 1877-1948; 2012-2016; 2041-2043; 2201-2246; 2270-2283; 2351-2400 (_Compendium_ questions 401-414; 428-433)

Further reading:
BIANCO, E., _Being a Christian_, CTS; SARKISIAN, R., _Life Work_, Ignatius Press; PELL, G., _Issues of Faith and Morals_, Ignatius Press; GASPARINO, A., _Sexuality and love_, CTS; CTS Explanations: _Contraception and Chastity_; _Homosexuality_; _Cloning_, _Infertility_; _Euthanasia_; _Abortion_; _Gift of Life and Love_, _Prenatal Tests_ ; WOODGATE, M., _A Rule of Life_, CTS

The Life of Prayer

The raising of one's mind and heart to God or the requesting of good things from God.

St John of Damascus, *De fide orth.* 3, 24

eVANGELIUM

What is Prayer?

Prayer is speaking and listening to God and desiring to be united with God and to do his will.

Why do we pray to God?

- We pray because he *is* God. It is therefore right to adore him, thank him and repent before him.

- We also pray because he listens to our prayers and will act on our behalf when we pray.

- We also pray to come to know God personally and this is our greatest happiness.

The principal activities of prayer

Christian prayer involves one or more of the following actions before God.

THE PRINCIPAL ACTIVITIES OF PRAYER	
Adoration	An act offered to God, such as a psalm of praise or a sacrifice which acknowledges his supreme perfection and our dependence.
Thanksgiving	An expression of gratitude to God for his bounty in satisfying our general or particular needs and especially for his gift of grace.
Repentance	A recognition of the wrong we have done to God by sin, a detestation of the evil effects of sin and a desire to turn from evil and do good.
Petition and Intercession	The asking of proper gifts or graces from God, such as material, moral and spiritual goods and protection or rescue from evils. Petition is for oneself; intercession is for others.

The Virgin in Prayer by Sassoferrato

Mistaken ideas about prayer

IS PRAYER JUST IN THE MIND?

Prayer is not just in the mind. God acts when we pray and frequently causes miraculous changes in ourselves and in the world.

DOES PRAYER SEEK A MENTAL VOID?

Prayer is not a mental exercise to empty the mind, as in Zen Buddhism or yoga. Prayer always has God and the things of God as its focus.

IS PRAYER JUST A TECHNIQUE?

Prayer is never a ritual technique like magic, simply seeking power or other benefits. Christian prayer leads to the knowledge and love of God.

*Rejoice always, pray constantly, give thanks in all circumstances;
for this is the will of God in Christ Jesus for you.*

1 Thessalonians 5:16 – 18

How Do We Pray?

VOCAL PRAYER

The mental activity of prayer joined to the physical one of words and gestures. Examples are the *Our Father,* the *Hail Mary,* the *Sign of the Cross* and grace before meals.

LITURGICAL PRAYER

The official and public prayer of the Church, such as the Mass or the Divine Office. It involves the Church as a whole rather than individual Christians alone.

MEDITATIVE PRAYER

Mental conversation with God often facilitated through Scripture, other holy writings and images that reveal him and his works.

CONTEMPLATIVE PRAYER

A simple and loving apprehension of God or divine things brought about by the Holy Spirit and the growth of his gifts in our souls.

Difficulties in prayer and their remedies

Prayer is not easy; the Catechism sometimes refers to the 'battle of prayer' (ccc. 2752).

☒ **No time**	Put aside time for prayer anyway. God will give our time back to us and will give success to all our good activities.
☒ **Boredom**	Persevere, turn back to God and perhaps try another kind of prayer. Learn more about what prayer means.
☒ **Distraction**	Avoid distracting places and times, but do not be too anxious about failure. God knows and rewards our efforts.
☒ **Dryness**	Do not make feelings the measure of success. God blesses those who pray even when they do not feel like praying.
☒ **No answers**	Persist and ask God to reveal his will. Sometimes he wants to give us something other than we have asked for.

The Meditative Prayer of St Dominic by Fra Angelico

What can help us to pray?

A regular time for prayer each day is a great help. It is also helpful to find a holy place, such as a church, or to set up a place of prayer in one's own home.

A Bible, Christian prayer books and devotional objects, such as holy pictures, a rosary and a crucifix, may also be of direct use in prayer or may help indirectly by establishing a holy place for prayer.

Who can help us to pray?

Christians pray by means of the Holy Spirit whose help we should always seek in prayer (Rom 8:26). We can also ask the saints to aid us with their prayers. In particular, we can ask our most powerful intercessor, Mary, mother of all Christians, to pray for us and with us.

We do not know how to pray as we ought, but the Spirit himself intercedes for us with sighs too deep for words. Rm 8:26

References

Catechism of the Catholic Church:
ccc. 2558-2758 (*Compendium* questions 534-556; 567-577)

Further reading:
KREEFT, P., *Prayer for Beginners* by Ignatius Press; DUBAY, T., *Prayer Primer* by Thomas Dubay, Ignatius Press; AUMANN, J., *Spiritual Theology*, Sheed & Ward; MARTIN, R., *Called to Holiness*, Ignatius Press

The Lord's Prayer

Lord, teach us to pray.
Luke 11:1

What is the Lord's Prayer?

The 'Lord's Prayer', also called the *Our Father*, is the prayer Jesus taught his disciples when they asked him to teach them to pray.

The Lord's Prayer is the most perfect of prayers, because it comes to us from Jesus Christ, the model and master of prayer. It is the prayer of the whole Church and is an essential part of liturgical prayer.

The structure of the Lord's Prayer

THE OPENING INVOCATION

Our Father, who art in heaven,

PETITIONS REGARDING GOD

Hallowed be thy name.

Thy kingdom come.

Thy will be done on earth, as it is in heaven.

PETITIONS FOR THE GOOD THINGS WE NEED

Give us this day our daily bread,

and forgive us our trespasses,
as we forgive those who trespass against us,

and lead us not into temptation,
but deliver us from evil.

The opening invocation

OUR

We pray 'Our Father', not 'My Father', because our common adoption as children of God establishes a familial bond among Christians. Jesus promises that prayer in common is particularly powerful, "*if two of you agree on earth about anything they ask, it will be done for them by my Father in heaven*" (Mt 18:19).

FATHER

We pray 'Father' because we have become children of God in Baptism. 'Father' expresses this relationship and the hope we have as his heirs, "*we are children of God, and if children, then heirs*" (Rom 8:16-17).

To pray 'our Father' is also to acknowledge that, as his children, we should imitate him and avoid the things that make us unlike him, "*You, therefore, must be perfect, as your heavenly Father is perfect*" (Mt 5:48).

WHO ART IN HEAVEN

We do not pray 'who art in heaven' as if the Father is 'contained' by heaven. Instead, this prayer recognises that there is a blessed place, the kingdom of heaven, prepared for us. There we hope to see God face to face and dwell with him forever; "*the Lord God will be their light, and they shall reign for ever and ever*" (Rev 22:3). Praying these words also helps to raise our minds to heavenly things and increases our hope of glory.

'Who art in heaven' also affirms that God is not simply a part of creation or the totality of creation.

Jesus Taking Leave of the Apostles by Duccio di Buoninsegna

"*In praying do not heap up empty phrases as the Gentiles do; for they think that they will be heard for their many words. Do not be like them, for your Father knows what you need before you ask him. Pray then like this: Our Father who art in heaven, hallowed be thy name. Thy kingdom come. Thy will be done, on earth as it is in heaven. Give us this day our daily bread; and forgive us our debts, as we also have forgiven our debtors; and lead us not into temptation, but deliver us from evil*" (Mt 6:6-13).

Run through all the words of the holy prayers (in Scripture), and I do not think that you will find anything in them that is not contained and included in the Lord's Prayer.

St Augustine EP 130, 12, 22, cited in the *Catechism of the Catholic Church* n. 2762

43

What are the Petitions?

The Agony in the Garden by Giovanni Bellini

Petitions regarding God

HALLOWED BE THY NAME

We pray 'hallowed be thy name', not to add something to God, which is impossible, but to pray for the wider propagation and growth of the personal knowledge and love of God; "*I have made your name known to those whom you gave me from the world*" (Jn 17:6).

THY KINGDOM COME

We pray 'thy kingdom come', so that God's present reign on earth might increase and his everlasting kingdom be established by Christ's coming in glory.

THY WILL BE DONE ON EARTH, AS IT IS IN HEAVEN

We pray 'Thy will be done on earth, as it is in heaven' because God is love and his will is for our good. God "*desires everyone to be saved and to come to the knowledge of the truth*" (1 Tim 2:4).

This petition teaches us that our freely offered prayers help to accomplish what God wills for us. Uttering this petition also conforms our wills to his, "*not my will, but thine, be done*" (Lk 22:42).

Petitions for the good things we need

GIVE US THIS DAY OUR DAILY BREAD

We pray 'give us this day our daily bread' to petition God for our natural needs. The original Greek word for 'daily' also means 'super-substantial' (as it is translated in the Latin Vulgate version of Mt 6:11).

Since the word 'super-substantial' indicates the Eucharist, this petition can be understood in two senses. We ask God to satisfy our natural needs and, above all, for the Eucharist, our supernatural food. In both senses, this petition counteracts pride by reminding us of our loving dependency on God.

> *The Eucharist is our daily bread. The power belonging to this divine food makes it a bond of union. Its effect is then understood as unity, so that, gathered into his Body and made members of him, we may become what we receive.*
>
> St Augustine, *Sermo* 57, 7, (ccc. 2837).

FORGIVE US OUR TRESPASSES AS WE FORGIVE THOSE WHO TRESPASS AGAINST US

We pray 'forgive us our trespasses' to petition God to forgive the debt of sin we owe him. Uniquely in the *Our Father*, however, the fulfilment of this petition is conditional upon a further action of our own, namely our willingness to forgive others. Jesus warns us explicitly, "*If you do not forgive others, neither will your Father forgive your trespasses*" (Mt 6:15).

This petition also reminds us that we *ask* for God's mercy rather than demand it.

LEAD US NOT INTO TEMPTATION

We pray 'lead us not into temptation' to ask God to remove temptations or to give us the strength to resist them successfully. Temptations encourage us to sin by presenting evil under the guise of good.

This petition also reminds us of our need to rely on God for victory against sin: "*This petition takes on all its dramatic meaning in relation to the last temptation of our earthly battle; it asks for final perseverance*" (ccc. 2849).

DELIVER US FROM EVIL

We pray 'deliver us from evil' to petition God to set us free from all evil and especially from 'the evil one', the devil. It is also a prayer of hope since it reminds us of God's power and desire to save us, "*If God is for us, who is against us?*" (Rom 8:31). Under the care of our heavenly Father, we need not be afraid.

AMEN

We pray 'amen' to complete the Lord's Prayer. It means 'truly' or 'let it be so'. It also expresses the expectation that God will grant what we have asked.

References

Catechism of the Catholic Church:
ccc. 2759-2865 (*Compendium* questions 578-598)

Further reading:
HAHN, S., *Understanding 'Our Father'*, Emmaus Road

Praying the Mass

Everyone is to examine himself and only then eat of the bread or drink from the cup.
1 Corinthians 11:28 NJB

*C*VANGELIUM

What is Praying the Mass?

Praying the Mass is the fully conscious and active participation in the Eucharist. This participation is prayerful engagement in the Mass, aided by proper understanding, good preparation and the application of its power and blessings to our lives.

Preparation for Mass

The Mass nourishes the Christian life, conforming us to Christ. Growth in the Christian life in turn gives us a deeper insight and love for the Mass.

We can also prepare for Mass in specific ways by meditating on the Scripture readings and by studying the structure and prayers of the Mass. It is also helpful to make the Sign of the Cross on entering the church, to genuflect to the tabernacle and to devote a period to personal prayer before Mass.

To prepare for Communion, we must first go to Confession if we have committed any mortal sins. We must abstain for at least one hour before Communion from all food and drink except water and medicine.

During the Mass

We participate in the Mass by being attentive, and by uniting our interior prayers to the words, actions and gestures of the priest. It is also important to:

- Respond and sing clearly, listen carefully, and try to understand what is happening.

- Remember God is present and receive the Eucharist with the greatest reverence.

- Realise the supernatural and miraculous dimension of the Mass.

After the Mass

After Mass it is good to devote a period to prayer. This prayer is a way to thank God for the blessings received and to ask for the strength to fulfil our new resolutions. It is important to foster an atmosphere of prayerful silence within the church at all times.

The Last Supper by Sassetta

Difficulties with praying the Mass

☒ **Makes no sense**	The Mass is rich in meaning and is unlikely to make immediate sense. Patience, prayer and study help us to appreciate its greatness.
☒ **Boredom**	The Mass is a prayer and something we need for our souls. It is not mere entertainment. However, in practice it will engage us deeply if we attend to the words and think and pray about what they mean.
☒ **Inability to receive Communion**	The Mass is primarily a sacrifice, and to attend Mass devoutly has great value even when we cannot receive Communion. We may still make a 'spiritual communion'.

The greatest help in overcoming difficulties is to appreciate that, in the Mass, we join with the heavenly liturgy spoken of in the New Testament.

You have come to Mount Zion and to the city of the living God, the heavenly Jerusalem, and to innumerable angels in festal gathering, and to the assembly of the first-born who are enrolled in heaven, and to a judge who is God of all, and to the spirits of just men made perfect, and to Jesus, the mediator of a new covenant, and to the sprinkled blood that speaks more graciously than the blood of Abel. Heb 12:22-24

O Sacred Banquet in which Christ is received as food, the memory of His Passion renewed, the soul is filled with grace and a pledge of the life to come is given us.

An ancient prayer of the Church cited in the *Catechism of the Catholic Church* n. 1402

The Structure of the Mass

INTRODUCTORY RITE	
Greeting: *In the name of the Father ...*	The Sign of the Cross commends the whole action of the Mass to the two central mysteries of the faith: the cross of Christ and the Holy Trinity.
Penitential Rite: *I Confess ...*	An opportunity to repent of our sins before listening to the Word of God and participating in the Eucharistic sacrifice of the Mass.
Gloria *Glory to God ...*	An ancient hymn of thanks, praise and triumph for our redemption.
Opening prayer *Let us pray ...*	With the whole Church, the priest offers this set prayer: a request of God the Father, in the name of Jesus and in the unity of the Holy Spirit.

LITURGY OF THE WORD	
Readings	The proclamation of the Old and New Testament Scriptures penetrates our minds and hearts, so that we can know God, his works and how we are to be saved.
Responsorial psalm	The prayers of ancient Israel that Jesus himself prayed.
Gospel	In the gospel we hear the words of Jesus Christ himself and what he did for us.
Homily	The homily explains some point of the biblical readings or teaching of the faith.
Creed *I believe ...*	The Creed is both a public profession of faith and a prayer.
Intercessions	The intercessions bring the needs of the Church and world before God.

LITURGY OF THE EUCHARIST	
Offertory *Blessed are you, Lord ...*	The faithful offer bread and wine, the elements Christ took in his hands at the Last Supper. These are the tokens of our sacrifice, which the priest offers on our behalf.
Preface and *Sanctus* *Holy, holy, holy ...*	These prayers give thanks (the meaning of the word 'eucharist') to God the Father for his work of salvation. They also remind us of the reasons for our gratitude. The *Sanctus* unites this thanksgiving to the eternal worship of the angels and saints in heaven.
Epiclesis	The priest extends his hands over the gifts, calling the Holy Spirit to sanctify these gifts, so that they may become the body and blood of Jesus Christ our Lord.
Consecration	The priest speaks the words of Jesus over the gifts, by which they become the body and blood of Jesus Christ ('**This is my body ... This is the cup of my blood**'). He elevates the host and the precious blood for adoration by the faithful.
***Anamnesis*, offering, intercessions**	The anamnesis brings to mind the Paschal mystery present in the Mass. The priest asks God to accept this offering of Christ himself and makes intercessions on behalf of the living and the dead, especially those for whom the Mass is specifically offered.
Doxology and Amen *Through him ...*	Lifting the host and the precious blood, the priest praises God. The acclamation of the faithful, *Amen*, is a triumphal assent and a conclusion.

COMMUNION RITE	
The Lord's Prayer *Our Father ...*	As well as being the model of all prayer, the Lord's Prayer expresses all the dispositions needed for the worthy reception of Communion.
The Rite of Peace *Peace be with you ...*	In the rite of peace the Church asks God for peace and unity, and the faithful offer the sign of this peace to one another.
The Fraction and *Agnus Dei*	The priest breaks the host as a sign that the faithful receive the one bread of life. The *Agnus Dei* ('Lamb of God') implores the mercy of Jesus, sacrificed for our sins.
Communion	The faithful are fed with the body and blood of Christ. They are united with their Lord, receive strength for their earthly pilgrimage and the pledge of eternal glory.

CONCLUDING RITE	
Final blessing	The priest blesses the faithful and sends them out on Christian mission in the world.

References

Catechism of the Catholic Church:
ccc. 1345-1355 (*Compendium* questions 271-294)

Further reading:
RANDOLPH, F., *Know Him in the Breaking of Bread*, Ignatius Press; HAHN, S., *The Lamb's Supper*, DLT

The Practice of Confession

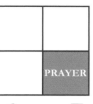

PRAYER

Forgive us our trespasses.
Luke 11:4; Matthew 6:12

*e*VANGELIUM

The practice of Confession is the means by which we receive absolution of our sins; the sacrament also helps us to avoid sin and grow in virtue.

When should we go to Confession?

We should go to Confession at least once a year, most fittingly in preparation for Easter. More regular Confession, such as once a month, is a great help towards spiritual growth. We should also go to Confession when aware of serious sin.

Parishes have set times for this sacrament, and often Services of Reconciliation, but a priest will also hear Confessions on request.

The Light of the World
by William Holman Hunt

Difficulties about Confession

☒ Fear	Both God and the priest welcome sinners with joy. The priest is bound by a seal of absolute secrecy. He will not be shocked by sins, and, as a sinner, goes to Confession himself.
☒ No sense of sin	Even the saints practised Confession regularly. A properly formed and examined conscience will give a true understanding of our sins (cf. 1 Jn 1:8).
☒ Unfamiliar	The basic formula is very simple and is good to learn. The priest will also guide those out of practice.

How should we prepare for Confession?

We should make an examination of conscience *(see overleaf)* to prepare for Confession, be truly sorry for our sins, resolve not to commit them again and to do penance. It is also important to pray before Confession and ask the help of Mary and the saints.

What should we be ready to confess?

We should be ready to confess all mortal sins. It is also important and good to confess any venial sins.

We need to confess the number of times we have committed each kind of sin, as well as we can remember (for example, *"I lied three times"* or *"several times"* or *"many times"*). We do not need to give any more details (such as names) unless something makes the sin more or less serious (for example, *"I lied to hurt someone"* or *"I lied because I was embarrassed"*).

A simple form of Confession

CONFESSION

Make the Sign of the Cross and say: **"Bless me Father, for I have sinned. It is** *(length of time)* **since my last Confession. These are my sins ... For these and all my sins, I am very sorry".**

PRIESTLY ADVICE AND PENANCE

The priest may then give some advice and a penance to be completed after the Confession.

ACT OF CONTRITION

"O my God because you are so good I am very sorry that I have sinned against you. With the help of your grace I shall not sin again".

ABSOLUTION

The priest will then give the absolution, by which sins are forgiven.

After Confession I should thank God and fulfil the penance the priest has given me. If I have accidentally forgotten to confess a mortal sin, I can be sure that the sin has been forgiven, but I must include it in my next Confession.

Penance requires ... the sinner to endure all things willingly, be contrite of heart, confess with the lips, and practice complete humility and fruitful satisfaction.
Roman Catechism of the Council of Trent, cited in the *Catechism of the Catholic Church* n. 1450

An Examination of Conscience

An examination of conscience is a systematic review of my life in the light of God's commandments. When preparing for Confession this examination should uncover all my sinful actions since my last Confession, especially any serious matters to which I have knowingly and freely consented.

	COMMANDMENT	EXAMINATION OF CONSCIENCE
1	**I am the Lord your God, you shall not have strange gods before me.**	Have I neglected to pray? Have I made any created things more important than God in my life? Have I engaged in superstitious practices such as astrology, fortune-telling, charms, spells, magic or the occult? Have I sought vain praise, failing to acknowledge God as the source of my gifts and talents?
2	**You shall not take the name of the Lord your God in vain.**	Have I deliberately given in to distractions in prayer? Have I abused or shown disrespect for any holy place, object or person? Have I blasphemed by using holy names, such as Jesus Christ, as swearwords? Have I broken a solemn oath or vow?
3	**Remember to keep holy the Lord's day.**	Have I missed Mass on Sunday or on a holy day of obligation without a serious reason? Have I engaged in activities on Sundays or holy days which have hindered the worship of God, works of charity or proper recreation?
4	**Honour your father and your mother.**	Have I refused respect or ridiculed my parents or religious superiors? Have I disobeyed my parents? Have I neglected my parents if they are in need? Have I disobeyed any other lawful authority? Have I made it hard for my children or others in my care to respect me by treating them badly?
5	**You shall not kill.**	Have I murdered or co-operated in murder? Have I assisted suicide (euthanasia)? Have I committed or co-operated in abortion (including the use of abortificient pills), IVF or the destruction of human embryos? Have I been involved in or supported an unjust war? Have I neglected the poor or needy? Have I quarreled, fought or hated anyone? Have I given way to anger?
6	**You shall not commit adultery.**	Have I committed adultery or fornication? Have I engaged in masturbation or homosexual acts? Have I used artificial contraception? Have I co-habited with a sexual partner to whom I am not married?
7	**You shall not steal.**	Have I stolen anything, including goods, information, money or software? Have I failed to pay my taxes and debts to others? Have I paid unjust wages or misled my employer by not working as I should? Have I failed to return borrowed property or make restitution for thefts?
8	**You shall not bear false witness against your neighbour.**	Have I lied about another under oath? Have I discussed others' faults and failings unnecessarily? Have I lied about or exaggerated the fault of another? Have I lied in any other way? Have I damaged the good name of another? Have I made rash judgments about another?
9	**You shall not covet your neighbour's wife.**	Have I desired someone else's spouse? Have I looked at or thought of others as sexual objects? Have I engaged in impure thoughts? Have I looked at impure pictures, read immodest literature, or used any other kind of pornography? Have I engaged in impure conversations or jokes?
10	**You shall not covet your neighbour's goods.**	Have I been jealous of another's possessions, talents or looks? Have I disliked another because of their achievements? Have I failed to thank God for his gifts to me?

References

Catechism of the Catholic Church:
ccc. 1422-1498; 2052-2557 (*Compendium* questions 296-312; 434-533)

Further reading:
A New Penance Book, CTS; RANDOLPH. F., *Pardon and Peace*, Ignatius Press;
O'SULLIVAN, F., *The Secret of Confession*, TAN

Catholic Devotions

Whatever you do, do it all for the Glory of God.
1 Corinthians 10:31

What are Devotions?

A devotion is a customary popular prayer, often linked to other holy actions, objects or places.

Catholic devotions are good because they help form habits of prayer, they are shared with others and they help to sanctify people, places and things. Their great diversity meets different needs and expresses some of the richness of the kingdom of heaven.

The Wilton Dyptich

The fourteenth century Wilton Dyptich illustrates traditional devotion to Mary. The panels depict King Richard II dedicating England as the dowry of Mary.

Devotions of the Liturgical Year

ADVENT AND CHRISTMAS

Advent is the four-week period of preparation for the coming of Jesus Christ, celebrated at Christmas. The most popular devotion during Advent in churches and homes is the **advent wreath**, with the progressive lighting of its four candles, Sunday after Sunday, until Christmas.

At **Christmas** it is customary to erect a **crib**, a devotion started by St Francis of Assisi. A crib is made up of figures of the baby Jesus, Mary, Joseph and others grouped according to the scene at Bethlehem where Jesus Christ was born.

LENT AND EASTER

Lent is the period of forty days in which we prepare, by prayer, fasting and penance, for the celebration of the death and Resurrection of Jesus Christ at Easter.

The most popular devotion during Lent is the **Stations of the Cross** (the *Via Crucis*). In this devotion we walk and pray at fourteen stations that retrace the Passion of Jesus Christ from his condemnation to his entombment. These stations can be found in nearly every church, and sometimes outdoors and at shrines such as Lourdes.

ORDINARY TIME

Ordinary Time covers the rest of the year. It includes, however, some major solemnities and feasts. On **Corpus Christi** it is customary to carry the Blessed Sacrament around the church or through nearby streets in solemn procession. On the **Assumption** we honour the Blessed Virgin Mary by a procession and by crowning her statue. The months of May and October are also times when we particularly honour our Blessed Mother. Many Catholics prepare for the major feasts by a **novena**, a series of prayers over the preceding nine days.

Devotions to the Holy Eucharist

EUCHARISTIC ADORATION

Eucharistic adoration is the worship of Jesus Christ, present under the appearance of bread. It is customary to expose the Eucharistic host in a monstrance for a set period of time outside Mass in order that we may see and adore him.

Most parishes set aside at least an hour a week for Eucharistic adoration. Another popular practice is the **Forty-Hour devotion** of the Eucharist, and in some places there is **perpetual adoration**.

BENEDICTION

Benediction is the rite of blessing with the Eucharistic host. It is given by a priest or deacon. It is customary to sing (for example, the *Tantum Ergo*) and incense the host during Benediction.

In the living tradition of prayer, each church proposes to its faithful, according to its historic, social and cultural context, a language for prayer: words, melodies, gestures, iconography.

Catechism of the Catholic Church n. 2663

Our Lady of China and Our Lady of Guadalupe

Devotions to the Blessed Virgin Mary

The Rosary is series of prayers which brings to mind 20 of the most important events in the life of Jesus and Mary. For each of the 20 mysteries (5 joyful, 5 luminous, 5 sorrowful and 5 glorious) we pray a 'decade', which is: one *Our Father*, ten *Hail Mary*'s and one *Glory Be*, following these prayers on a set of beads. We usually pray 5 mysteries at a time.

OTHER MARIAN DEVOTIONS

There are many other Marian devotions including the **Angelus**, the **Litany of Loreto**, wearing the **Brown Scapular** and the **Miraculous Medal**.

Devotions to the saints and the dead

PATRON SAINTS

Patron saints accompany, help and intercede for us. We choose saints as patrons, especially at Baptism and Confirmation. It is good to venerate holy pictures and statues of these patrons. Countries, occupations and activities also have distinctive patrons: St George is the patron of England; St Thomas More is a patron of politicians and lawyers; St Catherine of Siena is a patron of Europe.

PRAYERS FOR THE HOLY SOULS

A common prayer to aid the souls in purgatory is, *"Eternal rest grant unto them, O Lord, and let perpetual light shine upon them, may they rest in peace"*. To visit graves and pray for our deceased is a work of mercy.

Shrines and pilgrimages

SHRINE

A shrine is a church or other place of special devotion which, with the approval of the local bishop, is frequented by the faithful as pilgrims. There are many shrines dedicated to the life of Jesus or to a particular aspect of his humanity (for example, the Sacred Heart). There are also many shrines associated with apparitions of the Virgin Mary, such as at Fatima, Lourdes and Walsingham, and many shrines connected to the lives of the saints (for example, St Thérèse of Lisieux).

PILGRIMAGES AND VISITS

A pilgrimage is a journey to a shrine for the purpose of prayer and special intentions, the journey itself also representing the Christian passage through life to heaven. A pilgrimage can be short or long, and undertaken individually or in a group.

In a devotional sense a **'visit'** can be to a church to kneel and pray before Christ in the tabernacle. It can also mean the lighting of a candle and a prayer before a statue or image of Our Lady or a saint.

Recommended devotions for the home

PRAYERS IN THE HOME

It is strongly recommended that every Catholic family pray the Rosary together, pray before and after meals and at the beginning and end of the day.

HOLY OBJECTS AND PLACES IN THE HOME

It is fitting for every Catholic home to have a crucifix and some holy image of Mary or the saints. Some houses have a little shrine or prayer corner where a candle can be lit and prayers said. A family Bible set in an important position in the house is also a good practice. Many homes have a holy water font by the door of the house so that those passing by may bless themselves with the Sign of the Cross.

References

Catechism of the Catholic Church:
ccc. 2650-2696 (*Compendium* questions 351-353; 557-566)

Further reading:
GROESCHEL, B., *The Rosary. Chain of Hope* ; GUERNSEY, D.(ed.), *Adoration*, Ignatius Press; SOCIAS, J.(ed.), *Handbook of Prayers*, Scepter; *The Simple Prayer Book*, CTS; *Directory on Popular Piety and the Liturgy*, CTS

A Sequence of Teaching Sessions for RCIA

The following sequence of sessions supports those preparing for initiation and/or reception through the Rite of Christian Initiation for Adults (RCIA). The order can be adapted to personal requirements.

A Sequence of Teaching Sessions for General Education in the Catholic Faith

The following sequence of sessions is suggested for those who have already received the sacraments of initiation and who wish to deepen their knowledge and practice.

Pray for us, O Holy Mother of God, that we may be made worthy of the promises of Christ.